Snowshoeing

Snowshoeing

STEVEN A. GRIFFIN

STACKPOLE
BOOKS

Published by
STACKPOLE BOOKS
5067 Ritter Road
Mechanicsburg, PA 17055
www.stackpolebooks.com

Printed in the United States of America

10 9 8 7 6 5 4 3 2 1

FIRST EDITION

Cover design by Caroline Stover

Library of Congress Cataloging-in-Publication Data

Griffin, Steven A.
    Snowshoeing/Steven A. Griffin.—1st ed.
        p.   cm.
    Including bibliographical references (p.) and index.
    ISBN 0-8117-2928-1 (pbk.)
    1. Snowshoes and Snowshoeing I. Title
    GV853.G75   1998
    976.9'2—dc21   98-12787
                                                                              CIP

This book is dedicated to the memory of Gary Haske, a treasured, smiling friend who through decades shared with me the natural world in all its seasons. Your ashes have returned to your favorite haunts, your snowshoes are hung up. Still, Gary, we follow your trail.

14 95

Contents

Introduction

Each year I watch for the signs of approaching winter: crisp leaves fluttering to earth; chattering flocks of waterfowl preparing for journeys south; my dog puzzled by the thin skim of ice on his water dish.

Finally one day it happens. Water vapor molecules far above earth sublimate into frozen crystals that make their way downward. They fall on an earth's surface cold enough that they don't melt right away.

It snows!

The snow sticks, building to a depth that leads me to shed shoes and socks and head outside for a quick run around the house. The neighbors have seen all this before, and they ignore it the way I ignore their loud arguments, their trespassing kids, their curious habits.

This is my way of celebrating winter, with its cold, its ice, and especially, its snow.

Native Americans once also celebrated the first major snow of the season—with a dance. Winter to Native Americans meant hardships, but it was also the season when knowledge and tradition were shared among family and social groups drawn closer by the climate. With the right tools, they prospered in winter. The "welcome winter" dance featured the right tools, used to dance and honored at the dance's center. These tools were snowshoes.

This year my eleven-year-old daughter joined me for the barefoot run around the house in the season's first snow. Like my wife,

Mary Jo, Elizabeth has her own pair of snowshoes and uses them to enjoy the full long, snowy winter.

And so, the dance continues. Many snowshoes still look much like those used 150 years ago; others reflect the advances of modern technology. They're all practical and yet inspiring, lifting our spirits as they hold us aloft on the snow. They help us do what early residents of North America, as well as their counterparts in Europe and ancestors in Asia, did—prosper in winter and celebrate that season.

THE LURES OF SNOWSHOEING

I eavesdropped as one custom snowshoe builder was asked what lured him to the sport.

"Freedom," he said, looking off past a clump of pines to the snow-covered Utah mountain beyond. He cherished the ability to go anywhere he wanted, where many others couldn't, wouldn't, or didn't.

A second snowshoer I met on the trail that day asked if I was heading for "the tumble." Wildly energetic snowshoers had found a small slope down which they could run childlike, often as not pulling themselves from the powder after a somersault, dusted head to toe.

A sign welcomes visitors to join a snowshoe hike at Lassen Volcanic National Park in California.

A family returned from a hike—father, mother, and four-year-old daughter—vibrant with the glow of outdoor activity, having shared a winter adventure family-style.

My favorite snowshoeing consists of poking around in midwestern cedar swamps, visiting the haunts of snowshoe hares, bobcats, and slumbering bears, seldom encountering the track of a boot, snowshoe, ski, or vehicle.

Snowshoeing is all of the above and more. And it's so simple that, as many a snowshoe maker encourages the prospective buyer, "If you can walk, you can snowshoe." It's so practical, yet so exuberant and enchanting, that once you try walking on snowshoes you're almost sure to strap them on again. You may well feel the sentiment Florence Page Jaques shared in her classic 1944 book, *Snowshoe Country:*

> I love the deep silence of the midwinter woods. It is a stillness you can rest your whole weight against. Not the light silence of summer, constantly broken by the sound of leaves, birdsong, the scurry of little beasts, and the hum of insects. This stillness is so profound you are *sure* it will hold and last.

A wintry cap on a nest left from spring.

If that silence is to be broken, let it be by the satisfyingly squeaky scrunch of a snowshoe plodding along a trail, its wearer bound for some secret hunting or fishing spot; the rhythm of an athlete jogging along a path on lightweight snowshoes, her puffs of breath counterpoints to the whumps of snowshoe on snow; the soft giggles of adult and child alike in love with the winter world.

SNOWSHOE STATISTICS

Ski Industries America (SIA), a trade group that includes makers of skis, snowboards, snowshoes, and related gear, recently called snowshoeing the trendiest snow activity of the last eight years. In the first five years of the 1990s, numbers of snowshoers nearly tripled. SIA figures that about 640,000 people snowshoed in 1995, and many more joined them in the years that followed. In 1995 alone, about 150,000 pairs of snowshoes were sold in the United States.

An SIA survey reported in the *Detroit Free Press* focused on women who had given up downhill skiing. The most common reasons they gave were expense, family responsibilities, lack of ability, and time constraints. Welcome to the world of snowshoeing! This sport is affordable, fun for the whole family, easy to learn, and minutes away anytime there's a few inches of snow covering the ground.

WINTER CREATURES

The world of snow is called the *nivean* environment. Scientists have classified its animals into three categories, the names all stemming from *chion*, Greek for snow. *Chionophobes*, decreed A. N. Formozov, a Russian ecologist who broke the trail in snow study, are animals to whom snow presents a serious threat to survival. *Chioneuphores* are those that tolerate snow. *Chionophiles* have adapted to the snowy world and thrive in it.

The snowshoe hare is a chionophile. Its adaptations to winter life include its seasonal coat change to white and its oversize, snowshoe-like feet.

As in the animal world, so, too, in the human. The snowbirds who hustle down to Florida or Arizona are chionophobes. Those who spend their north-country winters in malls or cuddled up with books are chioneuphores. The winter people who have adapted to snow and thrive in it—the skiers, hockey players, ice anglers, and snowshoers—are chionophiles.

Atop the snow each winter, birds and mammals continue their food-gathering patrols. Within and beneath it, the beat of life goes on in other ways. There's food down there, in the form of fungi and dead and living plants. There also are small creatures ready to dine on that bounty, such as flies, beetles, and aphids. They, in turn, provide sustenance for beetles, wasps, and spiders, which are eaten by shrews and mice, which might perish in the jaws of a weasel. Thus the food web is intact in winter.

These creatures basically continue their habits year-round. The biggest change in their environment is the snow that hides them from our eyes, as well as those of the raptors, which as a result, have headed south toward easier pickings.

Animals have adapted to conditions such as snow over long periods of time and many generations, the very makeup of their bodies gradually changing. Some species have evolved seasonal adaptations. Feet of the arctic fox, for example, grow furry as winter approaches. The clumps of fur keep their paws warm and serve as built-in snowshoes. The ptarmigan trades its dark feathers for white ones that provide perfect winter camouflage. Feathers on its feet seem a likely inspiration for early snowshoe developers.

QUESTIONS OF DEPTH

How deep any creature—you included—sinks in snow depends on several factors. One is the density of the snow. This varies greatly from region to region, from snowfall to snowfall, and through the ever-changing nature of the snow as it lies flat on the ground in the accumulation we call the *snowpack*. It also depends on your weight—or, rather, how that weight is pressed onto the snow.

Biologists measure and compare the *foot load*, or *snow load*, of north-country wildlife, both prey and predator species. In four-legged creatures, that's one-fourth of the weight of the animal divided by the surface area of the foot.

The snowshoe hare has a foot load of about 12 grams per cm^2. The lynx pursues hares, aided by its own relatively low foot load of about 33 g/cm^2. The wolf's is just about 100 g/cm^2, near the average for a mammal of its weight.

Compared with the animal chionophiles, those that have adapted to and thrive in winter, we plunk down some pretty hefty loads on relatively small feet. The average human foot load, according to authors Halfpenny and Ozanne, is about 145 g/cm^2. We sink much deeper in the snow than does a snowshoe hare, lynx, or wolf. Without brains to devise technological help, our ancestors would have been hard-pressed to live in snow country. Maybe over a few million years, natural selection would have favored humans with bigger feet and smaller loads on them. We might all be shopping for size 22 Nikes today.

As in so many other ways, though, our brains carried us where evolution didn't. We cut our foot loads dramatically by making our feet larger with the addition of snowshoes or skis.

SNOWSHOEING STYLES

People use snowshoes in three main ways. Recreational snowshoers just like to get out on top of winter. Hard-core outdoor enthusiasts scale mountains or ski hills, headed for "extreme" sport. Racers and runners use snowshoes as an oversize version of running shoes, chasing fitness and performance.

People are rapidly joining all three user groups. Snowshoeing is reportedly the second fastest growing snow sport, ahead of alpine and cross-country skiing, and trailing only snowboarding. And some people combine sports, for example, hiking up hills on snowshoes and sliding back down on snowboards.

One reason for the impressive growth of snowshoeing is a new snowshoe technology that features smaller, lighter weight snowshoes with high-tech aluminum frames and synthetic decks— solid platforms of material in place of traditional laced webs. They make the sport a breeze to learn, with equipment that is reliable and

Jeff Sipola of Sherpa Snowshoe Company explains the sport to a visitor at a Winter Trails event.

nearly maintenance free. Traditional gear still works well, too; one of my favorite pairs of snowshoes is more than fifty years old.

Your world of snowshoes and snowshoeing can be as simple or complex as you like. You can step into the rubber bindings of a $100 pair of shoes and head out across a snow-covered golf course. You can match running snowshoes with exercise clothing and jog your way to winter fitness, thanks to this low-impact, aerobic activity. You can research the lore of traditional snowshoes, build your own, and walk on them to a winter campsite you'll remember all your life.

No matter what approach you choose, you'll undoubtedly feel a kinship with those chionophiles who, like countless other writers, north-country residents, and visitors, relish the quiet of the winter woods and the magic of walking atop the snow.

EASY ACCESS

Another reason for the rising popularity of snowshoeing is easy access to the winter outdoor world. All you need are snow and

The wintry world is open to the snowshoer.

snowshoes. More and more trail systems are being established across the United States, many of which offer snowshoeing. And many snowshoers take their first tentative steps atop the snow of community parks, two-track logging roads through state and federal forests, or even on neighborhood golf courses.

For some snowshoers, there's the lure of wilderness—backcountry where each visitor is responsible for his or her own safety, a trade-off for the opportunity to leave "no-trace" tracks in snow unblemished by other human footprints. Come a thaw or a few more inches of snowfall, no one will know you've been there, either.

Ski resorts have learned about snowshoeing's allure, and many now rent snowshoes and send visitors off on a different kind of adventure. Vail Associates combined forces with the Atlas Snowshoe Company to create a ten-trail snowshoeing system offering a variety of scenery and challenge in the Colorado mountains. The Giant's Ridge ski resort in northern Minnesota's Iron Trail tourism region hangs snowshoes next to its rental ski gear, and manager Craig Johnson, who also operates a sporting goods store in nearby Biwabik, said both his retail rack and rental hooks will hold more snowshoes next season. Similarly, rustic resorts often make sure pairs of snowshoes and trail maps are handy to their visitors, and some resorts even offer guided snowshoeing outings.

Blanketed in snow, places take on a special magic. Residents of deep-snow country take it for granted. Others among us, who know snow but not as intimately, marvel.

"It snowed 18 inches last night," says Russell Lesko matter-of-factly. The manager of Lassen Volcanic National Park in Northern California's mountains was accustomed to deep snow but knew his visitors might not be. "There's probably a couple of feet on the ground. We can get several feet at one time." Up to 800 inches fall there each winter. At the end of one recent winter, drifts up to 47 feet deep blocked roads at 8,500 feet elevation.

What is it about this snowy world that draws eager staffers, snowshoers, and skiers? "The nature and wilderness peace," Lesko says. "The serenity. You're away from all mechanization and motors. It's completely different than in the summer. And it's important to

Craig Johnson, rental manager at Giant's Ridge near Biwabik, Minnesota, adjusts a snowshoe binding to a renter's boot the easy way— without the foot in the boot.

have areas like this, where you can go and enjoy serenity." Important, too, to have snowshoes to take you there.

Many state and national parks offer snowshoeing programs. Quinn Rankin, a ranger at Lassen Volcanic National Park, coordinates a program that brings in kids for a lesson on winter and a taste of snowshoeing. Snowshoe walks with schoolchildren are held three days a week, with forty to ninety kids on each outing.

A small snowshoer gets a little binding help.

Program goals are to introduce kids to the world of winter, and to make it a world they care about.

"Our goal is for the kids to have a good time," Rankin says. "What we do depends on the size of the group and what the teacher wants—winter ecology, winter survival. We have them dig their own snow shelters, and they love that."

The equipment shed is stuffed with Sherpa aluminum frame snowshoes. Kids don't use poles. "Keeping track of the snowshoes is tough enough," she says with a laugh. The kids laugh, too. "In twenty minutes the kids can have snowshoes on and be heading up and down the hill, laughing and falling all over the place. It's a new experience, especially for kids from the valley, from places that don't have snow. Their eyes get really big."

On Saturdays during the snow season, snowshoe walks are also held for the general public. Other groups can be hosted by special arrangement.

A couple planning to buy snowshoes returns from a trial run during a Winter Trails event held by local sponsors, the American Hiking Society, and snowshoe manufacturers.

Some national park facilities, such as Bryce Canyon National Park in Utah, loan out snowshoes in exchange for the borrower's driver's license. In snow country, you can also check out ski resorts or equipment shops for snowshoe rentals.

In many places, community organizations such as colleges, recreation programs, and park facilities are getting into snowshoeing in a big way, offering workshops, snowshoe demonstrations, clinics, and races.

Other groups are also interested in getting you onto snowshoes. In February 1997 the American Hiking Society (AHS) launched a Winter Trails Program, in which snowshoe clinics were held across the country, sponsored cooperatively by AHS, local trail groups, and snowshoe manufacturers. Lessons were taught on both equipment and technique.

Snowshoes bridge the gap between the practical and the romantic, doing yeoman work carrying people atop winter, while igniting in their souls a passion for the snowy world.

Snowshoe History

Too often we think of winter as something to overcome. People didn't always see it that way. Ruth Kirk, in her delightful book, *Snow,* notes that the concept of snow as some kind of novel challenge is relatively new, just a few generations old. Before that, people just accepted winter and snow as part of life, and saw the advantages as well as the problems they posed.

And snow did offer some advantages. Getting around on an even surface of snow was often much easier than moving over lowlands, tangled brush, or other tough cover. "Webbed snowshoes in America and wooden skis across Eurasia made winter by far the easiest time of the year for travel," Kirk writes. No longer were people limited to established trails and waterways. They could move in any direction they wished, held aloft by winter's blanket.

ANCIENT SNOWSHOES

Nobody is sure just where snowshoes and skis were invented, or exactly when. The best evidence shows that they likely were developed in central Asia as long ago as 6,000 years, perhaps more. The two trace their roots to similar sources, what some have called simple "foot extenders," and they have been similar in their evolution.

Early histories had a rather generic definition of snowshoes. R. B. Orr wrote in 1920, "Snowshoes are of two kinds: first, those of wood—the *skee* or its equivalent; secondly, the netted snowshoe."

Generally, footgear made of wooden planks—skis—took hold and were further developed in Europe. Webbed footgear that became the snowshoes we recognize became most popular first in Siberia, then in North America.

Today, with cross-country skis available in wider models for more snowshoe-like loft in untracked areas, and with slimmer snowshoes made with solid fabric decks and fitted with cross-country ski and snowboard bindings, Nordic skis and snowshoes seem much more like cousins in the same tight-knit family than distinct winter tools of their own.

Their joint history is rich. The Greek historian Strabo, writing at about the time of Jesus' birth, described Asian natives who strapped on "pointed shoes made of raw ox-hide and broad as a drum." They'd climb mountains that remained snow-covered in summer and slide back down sitting on skins or sleds, in a technique that sounds quite similar to modern backcountry snowboarding. "Nothing is more rapid and more agreeable than this way of coming down the mountain," another historian wrote.

Snowshoes had more serious assignments, too. Soldiers of Alexander the Great crafted hoops webbed with rushes and used them to move easily over snow as deep as 16 feet.

Siberian snowshoes were made of white birch shaved to a thickness of $1/4$ inch. Those snowshoes or, more accurately, skis were about 6 feet long and 8 to 10 inches wide. On their bottoms were skins from elk, deer, or horse legs, placed so that the natural grain of the hair pointed backward. Moving forward, the skins slid easily over the snow. They made the footgear less likely to slide backward, though, a technological advantage for climbing that is still used by cross-country skiers in mountainous areas.

SNOWSHOES IN THE NEW WORLD

Webbed or plank, skinny or round, snowshoes or skis carried explorers from central Asia into Siberia and Scandinavia. Ancestors of the Native Americans probably used snowshoes to trudge across the then-exposed Bering Strait, following migrating game onto the continent of North America. By the time Europeans arrived in North America, Native Americans had long since developed webbed snowshoes crafted to perfectly suit the environment of the snowy north woods. Snowshoes were, in fact, the only way to move across North American snow until the 1800s, when emigrating Finns and Swedes brought skis to this continent with them.

Snowshoes were made in several shapes, with names that differed from maker to maker and from place to place. Frances Densmore, one of the first ethnologists to collect and preserve in writing the heritage of Native American peoples, reported the Chippewa or Ojibwa using three main styles of snowshoes, and sometimes a fourth. Round, "bear paw" snowshoes were standard. Longer, tailed snowshoes, called "beavertails," were used in two styles: flat, for travel in level country, and with upturned toes, better in wooded areas. A fourth style, less often seen, was an all-wooden snowshoe.

Densmore, writing in 1929 for the American Bureau of Ethnology within the Smithsonian Institution, said the round design, probably the oldest, was also called the "old woman's shoe." "The shape of these snowshoes is not unlike that of a bear's footprint," she wrote, "and the name also refers to an old legend that the bear once wore snowshoes. The second name is due to the fact that old women usually wear this kind of snowshoes."

The beavertail snowshoe has a round nose, and its frame ends in a long tail. They are usually 4 or 5 feet long, although they have been made as long as 7 feet. With their tail, these snowshoes tend to track well, aiding travelers moving long distances in a straight line across open country. The round, tailless bear paws, however, made changing direction easier, a plus when moving through heavy brush.

From these two basic designs—bear paws and beavertails—evolved dozens of variations, each of which best matches a certain set of environmental conditions, as well as the size and needs of its owner. That was the case when the Native American snowshoe styles were developed, and it's still the case today.

With the snowshoe, the match of tool to need was nearly perfect. R. B. Orr, writing in 1920, said, "In the snow-clad land of our northern hemisphere, with its long winters and its soft snow, feathery and often many feet in depth, no equipment for the feet could be more serviceable than the snowshoe."

Many Native American tribes used snowshoes. Orr reported their use among Algonquins in Ontario, Iroquois in the southern Great Lakes region, and arctic Eskimos. Cree were said to use snowshoes for both waging war and hunting, and Arapaho to use oval snowshoes in their winter pursuits of buffalo. Jesuit explorers and missionaries described natives' use of both snowshoes and the moccasins worn with them.

"The moccasin is as necessary an appendage to the snowshoe as the paddle is to the far-famed birch-bark canoe," Orr wrote. Before pulling on moccasins, the Native American snowshoer wrapped his or her feet in rabbit skins, moose hair, or other pelts—an early version, it seems, of our wool felt liners.

Snowshoe and moccasin making was women's work, and construction methods varied by maker and materials available. Frames might be of willow, ash, spruce, box elder, or maple. A long stick, about 1/2 inch in diameter, was bent into a teardrop shape, and the two ends of the stick were secured together to become the shoe's tail. The frame was 2 to 4 feet long and 10 to 18 inches wide, and was braced by flat, narrow strips of wood, one a few inches back from the front, the other about twice as far from where the two ends of the teardrop-shaped frame met.

"The interior of the frame," Orr wrote, "with the exception of a space about four inches wide back of the front cross-piece, is filled in by weaving thongs into a network whose meshes vary according to the design of the maker." Webbing materials varied. Hide was taken from several aquatic and land animals, including deer, moose, beaver, eel, and even horse, which, ethnologist Frances Densmore wrote approvingly, stretched and shrank little. The hide was fleshed, dehaired, and stretched until dry. Snowshoe web weavers used flat needles made of bone or antler. The needle had an eye at its midpoint, was rounded at each end, and could be used in either direction.

An opening in the webbing at the front of the shoe was created for the wearer's toes. Lashing bound the foot to the snowshoe, allowing the foot to rotate, the heel to lift, and the toes to extend into the opening as the wearer walked, sliding the snowshoe forward with each step.

The design was perfect for the task. "It is a very simple invention but exactly adapted to its purpose," wrote Orr. "A person accustomed to snowshoes can walk far more rapidly upon the snow than without them upon the ground. In hunting, especially, it is of the greatest service."

Snowshoes made hunting deer or bison relatively easy. Native Americans might lash on snowshoes and surround a herd of deer, driving the animals into a snowbank, where the hunters, armed with lances, could easily kill them. Buffalo could be pursued until mired, and then bow and arrow or lance could be used to kill the animal. George Catlin in the 1830s drew scenes of American Indians hunting buffalo while wearing flat, elliptical snowshoes.

"Hunting on snowshoes was so simple and safe," wrote Tom McHugh in his 1972 book, *The Time of the Buffalo*, "that even women and boys were able to bring down animals. The promise of an easy kill brought by the first big snowfall was celebrated joyfully among the Chippewas with a Snowshoe Dance. Singing gratitude to their spirit powers, the Indians clomped about on their webs, waving gaily decorated standards and circling around a post from which dangled a pair of snowshoes."

On their arrival in the New World, Europeans were quick to borrow snowshoe technology, as they did such other superb adaptations as the bark canoe, to aid their trade, hunting, surveying, and exploration efforts.

A Captain Knox wrote in his *Historical Journal* in 1759, "Our soldiers make great progress in walking on snowshoes, but men not accustomed to them find them very fatiguing. . . . A light lively man does not require them so large as he who is more corpulent and less active." At the time, the term *snowshoes* seemed to be applied to wooden skis and webbed shoes alike.

"The heaviest man whatever, with a pair of them, may walk on snow that would take him to his neck," Knox wrote, in a report today's honest snowshoer finds a little optimistic, "and shall not sink above an inch and a half or two inches; light men, who are accustomed to them, leaving barely their impression behind them."

Knox compared them favorably to the snowshoes of Siberia and Russia, which, from their descriptions, were cross-country skis. "Made of a very thin piece of light wood, about five feet long and five or six inches broad, inclining to a point before, and square behind . . . on these shoes a person may walk over the deepest snow for a man's weight will not sink him above an inch; these, however, can only be used on plains." For hilly areas, skin-equipped skis were used.

Snowshoe designs remained true to their roots—wooden frames bent into teardrop or oblong shapes, laced in a webbed pattern with rawhide. Gradually, as the land was settled, people began to use snowshoes for more recreational purposes. In the 1800s and early 1900s, snowshoe clubs were formed, especially in Quebec and eastern Canada and in the New England states, and people gathered for winter hikes, races, and parties.

Not all snowshoe history is so pleasant, however. In the winter of 1846–47, the infamous Donner party's eighty-nine people were caught by early-winter storms in the Sierra Nevada. Almost half of them starved to death; those who survived ate those who didn't. Finally, ten men and five women left the camp—on snowshoes—and headed for Sacramento. All five women and two of the men survived, thanks no doubt to the snowshoes.

And some bits of snowshoe history are amusing. On one antarctic expedition, explorers strapped round snowshoes to the hooves of mules to keep their feet from sinking so deeply into the snow. The snowshoes worked, even if the mules decided not to.

French speakers called the "snow rackets" they found here *raquettes,* and they still use that name today. Raquette Lake in the Adirondack Mountains is said to have been named for the footgear. Alan Mapes wrote in the *Conservationist* in 1994 that French and Indian soldiers running from the British in the mid-1700s threw their snowshoes into the lake when the winter's snow melted.

RECENT SNOWSHOE HISTORY

By 1906 Walter F. Tubbs was making snowshoes in Norway, Maine. Along with ash-framed snowshoes, he crafted skis, sleds, and snowshoe furniture. Tubbs's snowshoes were selected by Admiral Byrd's 1908 expedition to the South Pole. The company was sold and moved to Vermont, where it changed hands several times but continued building snowshoes.

A big surge in snowshoe making came with World War I, when the British government placed a large order for snowshoes for its troops. This led to a dramatic expansion of the Tubbs factory. By World War II the Vermont Tubbs company had been sold to American Fork & Hoe, which made hundreds of thousands of pairs of snowshoes for the United States and its allies.

Many snowshoe users were civilians, who often pursued trapping, hunting, logging, or other outdoor occupations. When World War II ended, thousands of pairs of surplus snowshoes were sold. Many of the rugged and high-flotation cross-country models are still in use today.

Trappers and other traditional users of snowshoes called the tracks left by a snowshoer a *beat,* according to a 1962 article by Edmund Ware Smith in the magazine *Ford Times.* Smith said that was because the path created was beaten down into the snow.

"Instead of telling his best girl he enjoyed her company, the trapper said, 'I'd like to walk in your snowshoe's beat.'"

Smith also warned his readers that they might feel sore in their lower shins from lifting the toe of the shoe to step forward. "The same ache was known to trappers who traveled immense distances on snowshoes. In the region where the ache occurred a swelling sometimes showed, and this was called *mal du raquette*."

These military surplus snowshoes have nylon-coated cable lacings, part of the military war on rodents, which often chewed through rawhide lacings.

Little changed in the snowshoe world through the middle decades of the twentieth century. The most notable change probably was the new option of neoprene, a synthetic rubber, as a lacing material. The military moved into snowshoe synthetics for one reason: Rodents, especially mice, loved to gnaw on the rawhide lacings. "The military had to stockpile tens of thousands of snowshoes, in case of a war, and rodent damage was a real problem," says snowshoe maker Jack Teegarden. Neoprene is more durable than rawhide, needs less maintenance, and is less palatable to rodents and other animals. Clarence Iverson is generally credited with developing snowshoe lacing of neoprene-coated nylon.

Snowshoe users debated the efficiency of neoprene versus the traditional charm of rawhide, likely unaware that far more radical changes were just around the corner. Snowshoe designers tried a variety of other materials for webbing and framing, but the next big change occurred in the 1970s, when lightweight snowshoes were developed using aircraft-grade aluminum alloy frames and decks made of solid pieces of fabric material instead of webbing. The result, according to Ski Industries America, was a lighter, shorter, narrower snowshoe that by the 1980s met "a general desire for aerobic, low-impact outdoor activities that were family-oriented and affordable." That modern shoe was developed in the West, where it became a nearly instant favorite because it so well suited the mountains.

Fitted with metal cleats, teeth that dig into the snow and ice, the metal-framed, fabric-decked shoe was great for climbing and descents. Its size and weight reduced the work involved in moving across mountain snows. Even in the East, still the heart of wooden snowshoe country, metal-framed, solid-decked shoes made fans of those who wanted light, small, low-maintenance snowshoes.

Soon, in a mirror of the snowy world of a century or so ago, clubs were forming, hosting hikes, races, clinics, and other ways to enjoy the wintry landscape. Groups, families, and individuals continue to discover that R. B. Orr was right more than seventy-five years ago when he wrote, "No equipment for the feet could be more serviceable than the snowshoe."

Bill Prater, inventor of the Sherpa snowshoe, which launched the modern snowshoe era.

Much of the growth in popularity of snowshoeing can be traced directly to the innovations in the snowshoes. As the American Hiking Society says, "Today's compact, feather-light snowshoes are more appealing, easier to walk on, and provide more traction than traditional wooden laced models of the past. User-friendly, the new binding systems offer more support, control, and ease of entry for all-terrain fun in the snow."

The man responsible for launching the modern snowshoe revolution was Bill Prater, a guy who liked to run around in the mountains on snowshoes. With his late brother, Gene, and a casual bunch who called themselves the Sherpa Climbing Club, he donned snowshoes and took to the mountains of Washington State. Most of their climbs were on military surplus snowshoes, the big, wooden-framed styles still seen on walls and snowfields across the North. I still walk on a pair sometimes.

Bill figured there had to be a better way to stay on top of the snow. While working for Boeing, he had attended engineering school. When he was laid off from Boeing, he intensified his snowshoe work, beginning with a binding designed to attach to traditional webbed snowshoes and provide sounder linkup of boot to snowshoe. He built them in his basement and traveled from shop to shop selling them.

Meanwhile, he studied the mechanics of aluminum, especially the alloy used so successfully in the aerospace industry. "I started playing with the framing of snowshoes with this strong, lightweight material."

The play turned serious. "A friend of mine, a metallurgist, had bought a bending machine. He insisted I take it, when he realized I was serious about my work on snowshoes. Through trial and error, I learned how to bend aluminum alloy tubing. The toughest was the compound bend at the end for the toes," a bend both inward and upward. "The deck was less of a problem. The early ones were less full than today's," and they had more lacing.

Prater first used neoprene-coated nylon to lace the neoprene deck to the aluminum frame, then even better materials as they became available. "We started with neoprene, slitting laces from a 500-pound roll. Next came extruded polyurethane." A secure lace-up binding and tough crampons completed the snowshoe. "The first models were basically the same as the current Sherpa Featherweight. There are some different features, but many of the sizes are still the same."

Sherpa still uses the modified bear paw shape Prater settled on, something of a rectangle with rounded corners. This shape boasts the highest flotation-to-weight ratio.

Prater perfected his snowshoes, getting the permission of his hiking buddies to use the club name Sherpa for the company. Serious snowshoers—search and rescue teams, mountaineers, and others—soon adopted them, but this modern vision of a snowshoe didn't really catch fire until the mid-1980s, when the fitness boom hit, with jogging and running leading the way. In cold weather, competitors toughed it out in marathons and contests such as the Mountain Man Triathlons, which combined cross-country skiing, skating, and snowshoeing.

"In Colorado," relates the Redfeather Snowshoe Company, "a few top racers on the winter circuit began to appear on smaller, revolutionary snowshoes and began to win regularly. They were wearing Redfeathers, designed by a fellow racer who hand-made them in Leadville."

The stage was set: Sherpa-style shoes for the mountains, Redfeathers for the races, and a population ready to embrace the winter outdoors in search of a fitter lifestyle. In less than a decade, more than twenty companies were making aluminum frame snowshoes in commercial quantities, and two-thirds of a million people were snowshoeing each winter. The numbers are still climbing at an astonishing rate. Meanwhile, four North American companies—two in the United States and two in Canada—continue to make commercial quantities of wooden-framed snowshoes, typically offering them in both rawhide and neoprene.

Snowshoes have continued to grow smaller as decks have replaced webs. New collapsible snowshoes fill smaller packages yet and are popular with snowboarders who want to be able to stash their snowshoes after scaling a slope, and with folks who want snowshoes handy but unobtrusive for emergency or adaptive use.

In a centuries-old tradition, a bowhunter stalks game in a snowy woods.

Snowshoe Principles

The principle behind snowshoeing is simplicity itself. We sink into snow—a fluffy and porous surface—because our feet are small relative to our weight. Snowshoes make our feet bigger, so we sink less. And using snowshoes is virtually as easy as walking itself, thus the process of learning to snowshoe takes only minutes, not hours, days, or weeks.

SNOWSHOE ANATOMY

A snowshoe has only a few main parts. The *frame* is the skeleton. It usually, but not always, includes both an outside framework and crosspieces that provide stability within. Most snowshoes have either a traditional, steamed and bent wood frame or an aircraft aluminum alloy frame that is welded or riveted together. There are also snowshoes made with plastic frames, and some injection-molded snowshoes in which frame and deck are one piece of plastic. Some snowshoes, particularly some military-issue snowshoes, are made with frames made of high-strength aircraft magnesium alloy.

Wooden frames must be made from wood that has straight grain and no knots or other flaws that might weaken it. Most wood-framed snowshoes are made of white ash, sugar maple, or yellow birch.

Some aluminum alloy frames are *anodized*, given an electrostatic coating that protects the aluminum from corrosion. Others are painted using an etching preparation to prevent chipping.

Decking, also known as carrying surface, is the surface that effectively makes our feet bigger. It may be webbed, as are traditional rawhide-laced snowshoes or their modern neoprene cousins, or it may be solid or nearly solid, as are many of the new-design snowshoes with neoprene or other synthetic decks. These new-style decks give excellent flotation. The same size snowshoe will provide much more flotation with solid decking than with webbing, and one can therefore wear a much smaller snowshoe if it is decked.

The *binding* attaches the foot to the snowshoe. Bindings come in a bewildering array of styles, from an impromptu harness fashioned of cord to a snap-in binding the same as those used for cross-country skiing or snowboarding and designed so that the wearer can switch from one to another in seconds. In between those

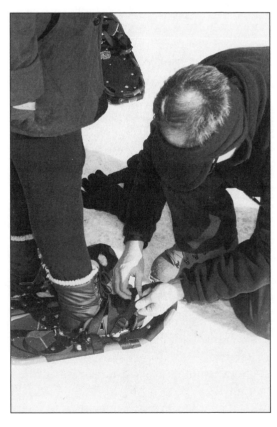

Assistance can make adjusting bindings much easier.

style extremes are A-type and H-type bindings, named for the approximate shapes their straps form. The A-type binding fits like a sandal, and the H-type consists solely of straps. These are good in neoprene as an economical, secure binding but are miserable in leather, which soaks and stretches. Rubber bindings with egg-shaped openings for boots are easy to use and are especially good for multiple users or multiple boots, or for the growing feet of children. They lack the side-to-side stability of other designs, though.

Some snowshoes, especially in the West, have *cleats* or *crampons,* metal teeth that dig into icy snow for better traction. Cleats are built into some snowshoes and are attached as options to others.

H-style bindings require occasional tightening on the trail. These are made of neoprene.

A young snowshoer shows what the bottoms of the snowshoes, including the cleats, look like.

TRACTION

Traction is the snowshoe's ability to resist slipping on packed snow or ice. Traditional webbed snowshoes provide traction through the webbing itself, each strap cutting into the surface slightly and then resisting sideways movement much like a car's snow tire.

Modern snowshoes achieve the same effect in different ways. Metal cleats attached to the bottom of the modern snowshoe provide good grip. Some are standard equipment on specific snowshoe models; others can be added as accessories. Heel cleats are particularly effective and popular.

Sherpa lashes the deck to the frame of some of its models with laces that wrap around the aluminum frame, providing great

A snowshoe racer usually runs on a groomed and packed trail and doesn't need much flotation.

traction. Other snowshoe makers also use webbing on the frames to boost traction. Tubbs has a line of aluminum frame snowshoes that have traction patterns molded right into the bottom side of the decking. Some entry-level, all-plastic snowshoes have serrated edges molded into them for traction and are even available with metal studs that allow them to grip like ice creepers.

Small snowshoers need only small snowshoes for big fun.

SNOWSHOE SHAPES

Snowshoe shape names can be traced to traditional snowshoe designs. They include *bear paws*, which are short and symmetrically oval; *beavertails*, which are wide in the center and tapered in back to a pointed, short tail; and *cross-country* or *Alaskans*, which are long and narrow, with a short tail, and differ from each other mainly in the amount of upswing in the toes.

There are many shapes in between these three, and there's often more than one name for the same basic style. Study the manufacturers' catalogs to help you make a decision.

Most modern aluminum-frame snowshoes are either symmetrical, in a slightly elongated bear paw shape, or asymmetrical for running and training. Running snowshoes don't look at all like traditional webbed snowshoes.

CHOOSING THE RIGHT SNOWSHOES

The purpose of snowshoes is to minimize the depth to which you sink in snow. The ability to do that is known as the snowshoe's *flotation*, and it's a direct function of the snowshoe's size, shape, and decking material. Snowshoes also help keep you moving across the snowpack by *traction*.

If size and weight didn't increase the effort needed to walk in snowshoes, we'd all strap on monstrously big snowshoes. But hikers often say a pound on the feet equals 8 pounds on the back, and snowshoers would be quick to agree. So you need to seek a balance—the smallest snowshoe that will keep you acceptably high in the snow. No snowshoe will keep you from sinking at least a little, unless you're on ice or thick crust. You need to balance the heft and size of the snowshoe against the snow you'll be traveling over, sinking in a little, but a lot less than you would without the snowshoes.

Several things make it difficult to choose the best snowshoe. Not all snow is the same. The snowshoe that will hold you on top of wind-packed, settled snow may let you sink a foot or deeper into cold, fluffy, new-fallen snow. Add a pack filled with camping gear or fishing equipment to your back, and the extra 20 or 30 pounds will help press your feet deeper into the white stuff. It's no wonder avid snowshoers often have a couple pairs of snowshoes, the better to match the conditions. It's not that the other snowshoes don't work well—it's just that the right pair for that day works so much better. And snowshoe fans, like boaters and other recreationists, always seem eager to find an excuse to expand their equipment collections anyway!

There's a whole world of snowshoe options out there, with about two dozen companies offering a full range of designs, materials, sizes, and prices. Snowshoes fall into three main categories: mountaineering, recreational, and aerobic. Within the category of your choice, look at the various models for the snowshoe that best suits your needs. To decide which pair will work best for you, consider the snow conditions and terrain on which you'll be using them; the combined weight of your body, clothing, and gear; aesthetics; and price.

The biggest practical distinction in recreational snowshoeing is between hiking through untracked country and following a trail that's been packed by others. The former requires a much larger snowshoe, the latter a much smaller one. Many experts recommend using the smaller snowshoe, even though you'll sink a little deeper in the snow when breaking trail. You'll have a much easier time walking on a broken or packed trail.

Whether larger or smaller snowshoes will work better also depends on the conditions. Wet or icy snow lets you get away with smaller snowshoes than you'd need on high-country powder. In open country, larger snowshoes will likely get the nod. In hilly country, you're probably going to need crampons for additional traction.

Traditional wooden-framed snowshoes sink in powder or loosely packed snow. Some people love the look of the webbed feet, however, and aesthetic considerations are part of their purchase decision.

Though top-of-the-line snowshoes may sell for $300 or more, there's a friendly batch of snowshoes, available for around $100, that are just fine for the golf course or local park. "The $100 shoe is acceptable technology for first-time snowshoers," says Ed Kiniry of the Tubbs Snowshoe Company. "I advise people to figure out how much they can spend, and to buy the best binding they can." It's the binding securing the foot to the snowshoe, Kiniry says, that represents much of the price difference and determines much of the ease and comfort of snowshoeing.

By investing a little more money, around $200, you can buy a much better snowshoe that will likely last a lifetime. When you move toward the $300 price point, many snowshoes carry a lifetime warranty.

SELECTING BINDINGS

When shopping for bindings, wear the boots you'll most often wear when snowshoeing. The bindings must be secure and comfortable. You don't want bindings so loose your foot slips out or so tight they pinch your feet, constricting circulation and making your feet get cold—maybe dangerously cold—quickly.

Hunters, anglers, and other winter sports fans often wear pac boots, which are very warm but quite bulky. They need bindings with large openings.

Runners can select bindings made to work with summer-style running shoes. Mountaineers, at the other extreme, can buy bindings that lock down tightly on their hiking boots. Snowboarders and cross-country skiers can wear the boots from those sports and step directly into the same bindings mounted on snowshoes. If you're going to be snowshoeing downhill, choose a binding that has an end cap to serve as a foot stop.

ROTATION

Rotation refers to the movement of the foot in relation to the ground and the snowshoe. The traditional webbed snowshoe, with its toehole ahead of the stout toecord to which the binding is affixed, is made so that the foot is lifted, toe-down, to take the next step. The freely hanging snowshoe is suspended, remaining generally parallel to the ground. The snowshoer slides the shoe forward and then steps back down onto the deck of the shoe. That process is called *free rotation*.

Some early snowshoes, notably some Native American and some World War II aircraft emergency snowshoes, were designed to act exactly like oversize feet. Attached securely to the wearer's foot, they were to be lifted completely off the ground with each step. Many modern manufacturers make snowshoes like this for special purposes, including running. This arrangement is called *fixed rotation.*

Free rotation works especially well in deep and powdery snow. Snow from the edges of the hole tumbles onto the snowshoe, from which it slides off as the snowshoer takes the next step, foot raised and snowshoe sloped from the foot to the ground. Some snowshoers also favor free rotation for climbing, since the shoe remains parallel to the surface being climbed, allowing crampon claws to dig in.

Fixed toe rotation gets the nod on packed and broken trails, where there's little chance of the snowshoe burying itself beneath the snow. You can back up easily, since you're not wearing an angled snowshoe that acts like a doorstop.

A friend of mine, Ed Elliott of Midland, Michigan, says he tried snowshoe running years ago on traditional snowshoes. "We kept running along and then tripping and falling on our faces. We thought it was because of weeds sticking up through the snow, but we finally figured out it was our toes poking down through the snowshoe and catching in the snow. Somehow we figured out we could lash our heels to the snowshoe, to keep our toes from pointing down, and that did the trick." Elliott and his friends had converted their free rotation bindings to fixed rotation.

Through the first half of the twentieth century, virtually all snowshoes featured free rotation. Redfeather brought fixed rotation snowshoes to the market in the late 1980s, and Sherpa claimed the best of both worlds with its patented Dual Rotation system in the mid-1990s. This system uses a cam that detects the weight of the snow and transmits varied resistance. If the snow load is heavy, the tail drags like a free rotation binding; if unencumbered, the snowshoe lifts with the boot for the easiest walking.

Traditional Snowshoes

Even people who venture onto the snow only on modern, aluminum-frame snowshoes still buy T-shirts and sweatshirts with drawings of traditional snowshoes on them.

For many people, especially those with a decade or more of snowshoeing experience, the traditional snowshoe was the entry point into the sport.

I was ten or twelve when I decided that what I really wanted for Christmas was a pair of snowshoes. In mid-Michigan where I grew up, we got several good dumpings of snow each winter, and it was a short ride up north to where really deep snow lay waiting. I dropped not-too-subtle, preteen hints.

Come Christmas morning, there they were: a pair of wooden-framed, rawhide-webbed snowshoes, Michigan models, a beavertail design 13 inches wide and 48 inches long. They were fitted with leather harnesses I later learned were called H-style bindings.

The day after Christmas, I stared at the sky and the bare ground, hoping for a blizzard. The next day, I was still staring. Weeks later, I'd just about forgotten about the snowshoes when a big snow came.

Out came the snowshoes, on went the winter boots, and my introduction to snowshoeing began. Like many other firsts in life, it's a wonder this one didn't steer me away from snowshoeing forever. Nobody had ever told me that snowshoes weren't designed to keep you perfectly on top of the snow, but rather to limit your sinking into it. Nobody was around to tell me to let the oblong

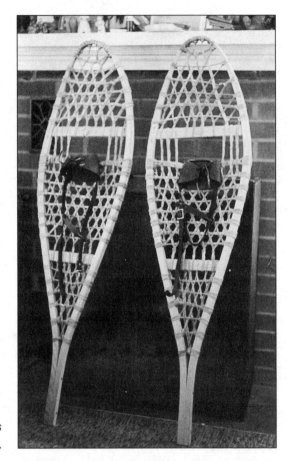

*The author's
first snowshoes.*

shapes interlock as I stepped, rather than holding my legs an
uncomfortable distance apart. And nobody had ever warned me
about leather bindings.

Those bindings were created by the devil, I quickly surmised.
Tugging as hard as I could, I could get them almost tight enough to
hold my feet steady and then begin walking. On the 30-degree F
days on which I did my earliest snowshoeing, the black leather
bindings quickly drew water and began stretching. Every ten minutes or so I'd have to stop and tug the straps to the next buckle hole.
If I didn't do that soon enough, my foot would slip completely out
of the binding and I'd have to reattach it, busting loose the strap that

remained tight but frozen, and then again trying to tighten the unfrozen, wet, and stretching parts of the bindings.

On my second outing I went prepared, a Scout jackknife in my pocket for poking additional holes in the strap, since it had by now stretched well beyond the factory-installed holes. I walked in some of the same areas I'd visited the day before and quickly discovered the big difference between breaking a trail and following one. I was learning to adapt to walking atop winter, albeit slowly and painfully.

Then came a stretch of several years when nature was stingy with snow and I was immersed in the pressing and mostly social concerns of teenage life. The snowshoes stayed in the closet.

A decade later, a huge snowstorm struck our part of Michigan, with one of the lowest barometric pressure readings ever recorded in the region. Winds rose behind the storm and piled huge drifts. Schools and businesses were shut down. Car traffic was virtually nonexistent, and the woman I loved lived more than 2 miles away.

Out came the old Michigan-model, Christmas-present snowshoes. I strapped them on, making sure I had a knife in my pocket in case the bindings needed more customizing. On top of snowdrifts as deep as 3 feet, I walked down the middle of one of the major streets in our town of 30,000 people and never once had to move out of the way of a car or truck. I did see a couple of cross-country skiers and a snowmobile or two.

I trudged through downtown Midland, then across a bridge high over the Tittabawassee River. Down a short road, up a driveway, and I was at Mary Jo's snowbound house, where I leaned the hardworking shoes against a cold fireplace hearth to dry in the room-temperature air. The bindings were soaked, and so were the lacings, a webbing material I would later learn was called split hide, an inexpensive lacing material quicker to soak up water than full rawhide. But I didn't care about any of that. These snowshoes had carried me to where I otherwise wouldn't have been able to journey. And the next spring, Mary Jo and I were married.

I now own several pairs of higher-quality traditional snowshoes, plus some fine modern Atlases, Sherpas, Tubbses, and other brands of snowshoes. Mary Jo has her own pair of Iversons. Our daughter, Elizabeth, has her own snowshoes, too.

But the no-name-brand Christmas traditional snowshoes, their leather-from-Hell bindings long since replaced by rubber doughnut-shaped ones, still hang in my home, occasionally taking a turn on the snow. They still have a place in my heart, for they were what made a snowshoer of me.

MAKING TRADITIONAL SNOWSHOES

E. Kreps, in his 1910 book, *Camp and Trail Methods: Interesting Information for All Lovers of Nature. What to Take and What to Do*, encouraged the snowshoe builder:

> A pair of good snowshoes will cost from $5.50 to $7.50, seldom less. If you do not feel like paying that sum, learn to make them yourself. While they will cost just as much in time and labor the average man can usually find plenty of time which would otherwise be unprofitably employed, and then he can see just what goes in the construction and can bring in all of the good points and eliminate the bad ones.

If you want to build your own snowshoes, makers such as Wilcox & Williams sell kits with instructions for making traditional snowshoes. Some nature centers and state parks offer workshops in snowshoe making. A nature center near my home has hosted snowshoe-making classes led by a Native American who used traditional methods and materials. Check with those in your area, and sign up early; these practical craft projects are often very popular. For most of us, however, a notion of how traditional snowshoes were and are made is enough to help us select and appreciate good ones.

There was a time, says wood carver and snowshoe builder Jack Teegarden of Atlanta, Michigan, when every village in snow country had its snowshoe builder, just as each had a blacksmith, a doctor, and a miller. Other villagers likely had the skills to build their own snowshoes if the need arose.

Teegarden, who no longer builds snowshoes for market but repairs heirloom and keepsake snowshoes on a custom basis,

Jack Teegarden readies a pair of traditional snowshoes for relacing.

describes the process as it was practiced in nearly every community in snow country. We'll refer to the maker as "he" here, although many accomplished makers and, especially, lacers were women.

First, the maker had to obtain and prepare rawhide lacing material. Often this was done well in advance, when the opportunity presented itself to obtain a cow, calf, or caribou hide or a few beaver or woodchuck skins.

The snowshoe maker would remove all meat and tissue from the skin and spread it on the grass, hair side up. He'd go to a fireplace in which had been burned hardwoods, not softwoods, and collect a couple of shovelfuls of ashes, mixing them into a 5-gallon bucket of water. He'd then work this thick slurry into the hair, roll up the hide in butcher paper, and bury it in sand for a day or two to let the lye work to loosen the hair follicles. Then, in the days before water quality was an issue, the hide would be lugged to a creekside, where the ashes and water would be rinsed from it.

The hide would be draped over a log and a dull, double-handled drawknife used to scrape the hair off it. The snowshoe maker would then secure the hide stretched tight to a wooden frame, on which it would be dried slowly in the shade. When finally dry, the hide would be rolled up and put away for later use.

When the time arrived to craft snowshoes, the builder would buy or cut some quarter-sawn boards, usually of white ash. Quarter sawing means slicing boards from the log as if they were spokes of a wheel, instead of the typical slabs cut clear through the log in sequence from the outer edge to the inner heartwood.

Eyeing the board, the builder would spot the grain lines, usually wandering instead of forming straight lines parallel to the cut edge. He'd use a band saw or other flexible blade to make a cut along the grain line, not the board edge, and a spacer to make a cut parallel to it at the width desired for the snowshoe frame.

The result would be a strip of wood with multiple S-shapes. Placed in a steamer oven for about an hour at 205 degrees F, the wood would straighten itself along the lines of the grain. Then it would be bent around a snowshoe form to form a teardrop or oval shape and any upturn in the toes. Most designs called for rivets at the toes. Mortised slats formed the front and rear crossbars.

The builder would especially watch the toe section of the frame during drying, as the severe and complex bend at the front of the snowshoe put extra stress on the wood there. Thick wood, because of the great difference in force between its inner and outer edges, sometimes begins to come apart under that pressure. According to Teegarden, the toes of thick-wooded snowshoes are wrapped in rawhide to absorb that force, whereas those with frames that are thinner in the toe area might not be.

Dried, the frame was ready for lacing. The snowshoe builder would take out the stored hide. He might tack a small block of wood to the top of a stump or bench and jam a knife next to it, point in the wood and blade angled into the cut, positioned a distance from the block corresponding to the desired width of the lace. This formed a jig, and the rawhide would be pulled through it in a spiral pattern. That would create a long lace. "With the flat helical curve, you can get 60 to 80 feet of lacing from a piece of hide the size of a large dinner plate," says Teegarden.

The lace would be soaked in cold water for eight hours to soften it, then pulled back and forth over the sharp 90-degree edge of a hardwood board. That stretched the lace and removed the curve from the cut. Again it would be soaked, and again stretched over the block. Now it was at its maximum length and was ready for lacing.

The lacing was applied wet to the snowshoe frame, and only at moderate tightness. When it dried it would shrink about 20 percent, creating a tight, supportive network on the snowshoes that was "drumhead hard."

Special knots and needles are used to lace snowshoes, and teachers such as Teegarden conduct workshops and classes in snowshoe making, presenting the variety of shapes, knots, lacing patterns, and other intricacies in this folk craft. In decades past, the village snowshoe maker knew it might be hard for you to tell your snowshoes from your neighbor's, so he would lace colorful woolen balls on the outside of the frames as an identification mark—"just like your mom may have done with a special fluffy ball on the top of a hat she knitted for you," Teegarden says.

Finally, the snowshoe was ready for covering with a coat of protective varnish. Today polyurethane is often used. But despite minor changes in materials, techniques, and tools, the process of making snowshoes has changed little since the days when frames were steamed and laces cut in every snow-country village.

PARTS OF THE TRADITIONAL SNOWSHOE

The parts of a traditional snowshoe have traditional names. The *master cord* is the main lace across the snowshoe, just at the back edge of the *toehole* into which the toe of the boot dips with each step. The master cord is the stout base to which bindings are attached.

The *front crossbar* stretches across the snowshoe ahead of the toehole into which the toe pivots during the step. The front and rear crossbars are wooden strips designed to give the snowshoe its shape, not support the weight of stepping.

Most traditional snowshoes have *frames* made from dried white ash, although other woods are sometimes used. The long-grained wood can be steamed and bent into a one-piece curved frame. Ojibwa model snowshoes are the exception, with two-piece wooden frames that have upturned toes and tails said to be great for moving through grass and brush, where pointed toes move the plants aside like a boat's bow does water, letting the wearer easily pass through.

The frame is drilled and lashed with rawhide or neoprene *lacing*. Rawhide is the traditional snowshoe lacing material. It comes in two forms, full hide or split hide. *Full hide* rawhide is made up of three sections: the top grain, the middle section, and the underside, or split hide. Intact, full hide is strong, durable, and more water resistant than split hide. *Split hide* is the underside, the meat side, left when the hide is divided to produce a high-quality top grain. Split hide is best used in widely woven snowshoes for beginner or weekend use.

Neoprene lacing, woven nylon covered with neoprene rubber, is strong, water resistant, and practically maintenance free. It doesn't stretch when wet, and snow doesn't cling, making the snowshoes lighter and easier to walk in. Whereas rawhide lacing dries to become tight, neoprene stays just the way it's laced.

Rabbit hunters and others who snowshoe in thick cover like short, wide snowshoes like these modified Michigan shoes, which are very maneuverable.

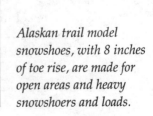

Alaskan trail model snowshoes, with 8 inches of toe rise, are made for open areas and heavy snowshoers and loads.

CARE OF TRADITIONAL SNOWSHOES

Traditional snowshoes, whether laced with full or split rawhide or neoprene, require more care and maintenance than modern aluminum snowshoes.

First, be careful to avoid excessive wear and tear or breakage. Walking across bare ground or icy snow speeds wear on traditional snowshoes. And don't use them as bridges between two objects. Snowshoes are made to spread your weight across the snow. Using them to span two supports is an invitation to breakage.

After use, traditional snowshoes should be dried at room temperature. Do not apply direct heat, and store them out of direct sunlight. And don't let wet snowshoes freeze. Store rawhide or split-hide snowshoes in a cool, dry place where rodents and other animals won't make a meal of them.

When the protective varnish shows signs of wear or when the rawhide lacing becomes limp while snowshoeing, it means revarnishing is needed. The friction caused by snowshoeing on an icy crust will peel the varnish from the bottoms of snowshoes, and once the lacings absorb water, they begin to stretch again. You get the "trampoline effect" of snowshoe decking that's too springy, says snowshoe maker Teegarden. He also favors smooth-bottomed boots that won't wear the finish off rawhide-laced snowshoes. His favorite pair, made by the Hudson Bay Company, have moccasin bottoms and are "absolutely treacherous" worn without snowshoes.

Neoprene-webbed snowshoes need less maintenance, but frames should be touched up with an oil-based exterior varnish when necessary. If the neoprene becomes frayed, quickly pass a small flame over the frayed area to fuse the strands together. Don't hold the flame in one place too long, however, or you may burn the neoprene material.

There may come a time when simply recoating rawhide-laced snowshoes isn't enough, and refinishing is necessary if you wish to continue to use them. Before beginning, however, make sure you really want to refinish them. Refinishing old snowshoes may cause them to lose any value that stems from their age. Teegarden owns several pairs of old snowshoes that he says he'll never rebuild—even though their lacings have been nibbled by mice—simply because he treasures their authentic look.

If you decide to refinish a pair of rawhide-laced snowshoes that you want to enjoy both on the wall and on the trail, Teegarden advises removing the bindings and then taking the snowshoes to a furniture refinisher who uses a high-pressure blower stripping system. "That blows off the old varnish and any mildew on the wood. When the snowshoes come back, they look like a brand new, unvarnished pair."

For a complete refinish, or to recoat snowshoes whose varnish has begun to peel, hang them vertically over a newspaper and paint on spar varnish or, better yet, polyurethane finish. Paint liberally so

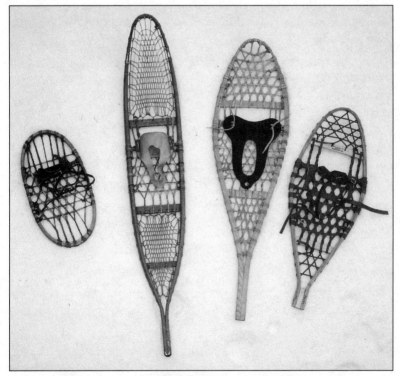

Four examples of traditional snowshoe shapes. From left: bear paw, Alaskan trail, Michigan, and Westover modified Michigan.

that the excess runs into the areas where the laces cross. Then turn the shoe upside down and repeat. You want the protective material to flow into every nook and cranny to keep moisture from seeping into the rawhide and causing it to stretch.

WALKING IN TRADITIONAL SNOWSHOES

Some traditional snowshoes call for slightly different pacing than modern ones. Aluminum-framed snowshoes can be placed next to each other when walking, like regular shoes. Long, slender traditional snowshoes can, too. But wide, teardrop-shaped traditional snowshoes require you to lengthen your step slightly so that the narrow part of the snowshoe strikes the ground next to the wide part of its partner, forming a zipper-like set of tracks.

It's been that way for thousands of years. It's part of the snowshoe tradition.

The Snowy World

Snow. White stuff. Winter blanket. Frozen water. That's what we walk on in winter, right?

Yes—and more. Snow is a seemingly magical substance that flies in the face of much of what we think we know about the laws of physics. It's as important for warmth as it is notable for cold. It offers both hardship and recreation.

There are people who seldom, if ever, see snow. But half of the earth's surface is snow-covered for at least part of the year, winter arriving on December 21 in the Northern Hemisphere, June 23 in the Southern Hemisphere.

Canada gets plenty of snow. In the United States, snow falls most generously along the West Coast and in the Rocky Mountains, Great Lakes Region, upper New England, New York, and Pennsylvania. Many other regions receive some snow, as well, and there snowshoeing can be at least an occasional pleasure.

WEATHER BASICS

Where does snow come from? Let's begin with a sketch of how weather happens. The sun is the great weather maker, putting all the ingredients of weather in motion as it sends its energy toward the earth.

Everything that pertains to weather comes down to the concept of *energy*, the capacity of being active or doing. Energy is neither created nor destroyed. It is transferred, from higher energy to lower, always seeking an even balance. Those transfers in our day-to-day environment often come in the phenomena we call weather. And the sun powers it all.

The sun warms the air, making it expand and become lighter. The warm air rises, while cool air shrinks and becomes heavier, and sinks toward the earth.

Earth isn't heated evenly, though. Our planet spins on an axis that's tilted. We're always leaning, in relation to the sun. As the earth rotates around the sun on a roughly 365-day schedule, one end points more directly at the sun for half of the year, less directly the other half. That gives us our seasons.

It's common to think of the earth in winter as tipped and at its farthest distance from the sun. Actually, our orbit around the sun is elliptical, and the planet is closest to the sun in January, farthest from it in June. It's the tilt away from the sun that creates our seasons, as it results in less *insolation*, or incoming solar radiation. Less of the sun's energy reaches us.

Sunlight passing through the cold air at the poles is weakened a bit because it has to pass through thicker, denser air, but more so because the sun's rays are more spread out by the time they reach the earth.

Aim the beam of a flashlight directly downward on a surface and it shines a small, bright circle. Aim it at an angle and the illuminated area is egg-shaped, larger, and dimmer. The same amount of light is being sent by the flashlight, but less of it reaches any one spot on the surface. That's winter sunlight, as our end of the earth is tipped away from the sun. Summer brings the concentrated beam.

Sunlight is always more spread at the poles—in summer and in winter—and so polar air is always cooler than at the equator, where sunlight is always more focused. That keeps warm air rising from the equator, cool air sweeping in from the poles to replace it. If the earth stood still, our winds would almost always be from the north. But it spins, and the spinning earth, like a gear in a machine, brings some of the moving air along with it. That creates the prevailing westerly winds of the Northern Hemisphere.

Pressure, another weather-making phenomenon, is also created by the sun. Equatorial air weighs less and is quicker to rise. That creates lower air pressure at the surface. The reverse happens at the poles, creating high pressure.

Features such as lakes, plains, and especially mountains create local changes in weather. In Michigan and many other Great Lakes states, lake-effect snow produces much of our winter fun.

Nature tries to balance the temperature and pressure differences, equalizing the energy. This happens on both large and small scales and produces what we call weather.

WATER WONDERS

Air is a mixture of gases, which include water vapor. All water molecules, water vapor included, consist of one oxygen atom wedded to two hydrogen atoms. The amount of energy in each water molecule determines its state: Low-energy water is frozen, medium-energy water is liquid, and high-energy water is vapor.

Water molecules slip relatively easily from vapor to liquid to solid, and each change can have a major effect on the earth's creatures, including us. These changes bring about the rain, sleet, hail, and snow that fall to earth, nourishing all life here. Heat, pressure, wind, and water mix and churn to produce weather. Among the many components of weather is the one we're especially interested in: snow.

Even before it's sent earthward, water exists in three states in the atmosphere: solid water, in the form of ice, sleet, snow, hail, or frost; liquid water, in the form of fog, dew, or rain; and water vapor, in the form of humidity.

Clouds are made of liquid and frozen water—tiny water droplets, tiny ice crystals, or, often, both. As these combine, they fall as rain, freezing rain, hail, or snow, sometimes changing form on the way down.

The change of water from liquid to vapor is known as *evaporation*. Warmth speeds evaporation, increasing the energy level and molecular movement. Lower air pressure also speeds evaporation. Evaporation requires energy, in the form of heat.

Condensation is the reverse of evaporation, changing water from vapor to liquid. And whereas evaporation requires heat, condensation releases it.

Snowshoers cross a snow-covered lake.

Sublimation is the changing of water from solid to gas or gas to solid, without the liquid state between. Sublimation is the process that makes snow.

Snow is not frozen rain. It's water vapor sublimated directly into ice crystals that form snowflakes. Ice pellets, sleet, and hail, on the other hand, all begin as rain that freezes as it passes through cold air.

If liquid water simply froze at temperatures of 32 degrees F and below, things would be relatively simple. But it doesn't. It generally needs a particle of some kind on which to begin building its crystalline structure, whether as ice from liquid water or snow from water vapor. Only when it reaches a chilling -40 degrees F will it freeze on its own. This particle, known as a *condensation nucleus,* might be a speck of airborne sea salt or a bit of sand or dust blown into the air. Even a bit of snow or water broken loose from a larger one during its descent toward the earth can serve as the nucleus of a new flake or drop.

Water that remains vapor or liquid below 32 degrees F is called *supercooled,* and it just waits for some particles to get the freezing under way. When those particles become available, either naturally or through cloud *seeding,* the hail, freezing rain, or snow begins.

A few particles mixed into a cloud of supercooled water can launch a snowstorm, experts say.

Once a few individual crystals of snow form, other molecules of water vapor attach themselves as crystals, forming a flake. A snowflake is a collection of many connected crystals, maybe even a thousand or more. Some crystals may break off from a flake, becoming condensation nuclei for other flakes.

Snow crystals begin falling with their flattest surfaces parallel to the ground and often rotate as they fall toward the earth. That puts them in contact with the maximum amount of water vapor, and they act as condensation nuclei for additional water molecules and thus grow larger.

FORMS OF SNOW

Snowflakes are made of full crystals and broken crystals cold-welded together, sometimes by the thousands, and sent wafting to earth. Most are only 1/8 inch or so, although they can measure up to 3 inches across. The biggest flakes form and fall in the warmest air. At the pole, where air is truly frigid, snow falls as tiny flakes, or even as individual crystals sometimes called "snow dust."

The shape of a snowflake is determined by the temperature of both the air in which it forms and that through which it passes. In 1951 an International Commission on Snow and Ice established seven basic classifications of snow crystals. The most familiar shape, the star-shaped snowflake of greeting cards, is the *stellar crystal*. A *plate crystal* is hexagonal. A *column* features hollow crystals. A *capped column* has a hollow core but is closed off at each end. A *needle* is a length of solid crystals. A *spatial dendrite* is a three-dimensional crystal. Any snowflake that doesn't fit into one of these categories falls into the *irregular* snowflake category.

Crystals and flakes don't stay in one shape for long. They gather water vapor molecules as they fall, and they lose edges and corners as they bump into each other on the descent.

Other forms of frozen precipitation include ice pellets, hail, and small, hard pellets called *graupel*, which are snow crystals heavily coated with rime, or liquid moisture gathered from the air as the snow falls.

SNOWSTORMS

Snow falls in flurries, showers, storms, and blizzards. Of them, the blizzard is the most impressive.

A typical blizzard begins when a low-pressure system moves in and dumps a lot of snow. The storm passes, and the snowfall usually stops. Behind it all comes cold air, high pressure, and wind. The winds build as the temperature quickly drops, and the already-fallen snow is picked up by the wind and blasted across the landscape. A snowshoer often can't tell if it's still snowing or just blowing, and it really doesn't matter very much; it's windy, snowy, and mighty cold. If there's enough snow in the air, a *whiteout* occurs, in which the air is so full of snow it's impossible to see more than 10 feet or so.

To be whalloped by a real, official blizzard, a region must experience low or quickly falling temperatures, winds of 39 miles per hour or more, and driving snow, falling or picked up from the ground.

Most winter storms aren't blizzards, though, and they follow fairly predictable paths, bringing ashore moisture from the Pacific Ocean, which falls as snow in the Cascades and Sierra Nevada, and retaining just enough moisture to dump a few feet of dry, powdery snow on the Rockies. Drained somewhat of moisture and energy, the storm starts rebuilding on the Great Plains, drawing in warm, moist air from the Gulf of Mexico and cold, dry air from Canada. It heads east, full of fresh moisture and energy and ready to hit the Midwest and Northeast. It may remain a winter storm or build into a blizzard.

SNOWPACK

When snowflakes reach the ground, if the ground is cold enough, they begin to pile up. Snow lying in a winter blanket is mainly air. Fluffy snow may be only 8 percent water and 92 percent air. Wind can also press snowflakes together on the ground, creating a firm snowpack rather than a fluffy one.

Snow changes dramatically once it's on the ground. This metamorphosis can take several forms. If the air and the ground are roughly the same temperature, *equitemperature metamorphism* takes place. Water molecules sublimate, or change directly from ice to vapor, at the points of star-shaped crystals. They sublimate again, this time from vapor back to ice, in the notches at the center of the crystal. Wind speeds the process. The crystal becomes smaller and harder with time. The snowpack settles and becomes denser, what scientists call "old snow." The snowpack itself is stronger. This is the most common process in eastern areas.

Even when the snowpack has become several feet deep, you can still enjoy snowshoeing.

Temperature-gradient metamorphism occurs when there's a large difference between snowpack surface and ground temperatures. It's common in the Rocky Mountains and other western mountain areas, where the air temperature is often much colder than the ground temperature. Water vapor from sublimation deposits itself on the outer points of the snowflake instead of the center, forming extensive glass-like, crystalline shapes. These beautiful flakes are often called *depth hoar,* and since they don't hold on to each other well, they produce an unstable snowpack. On steep slopes, they can break loose in avalanches.

The third type of snow change is *melt-freeze metamorphism,* or *firnification.* Sunlight melts the surface of the snowpack, and the meltwater moves down into it, where it refreezes at night. *Firn*—hard, firm snow that still has spaces between grains—forms from old snow. Glacial ice, from which the air has been pressed, comes next.

Snow reflects much of the solar energy that strikes it. It stays cold as night falls, and then radiates heat during the long night. The result is a net loss of warmth. If snow didn't provide some insulation for the earth, the loss would be much greater.

NAMES FOR SNOW

We tend to consider snow as a simple substance. Other peoples, whose lives are intertwined more intimately with frozen water, certainly know better.

The Inuit, or Eskimo, have many words to describe the various forms of snow. Some have been adopted by European and American snow scientists. *Api* is snow that has fallen but has not yet been moved by the wind. *Upsik* is snow that the wind has moved, shaped, and left in a firm mass. *Siqoq* is the snow in between the two states—moving along the ground. American Indians in Alaska, similarly, have created words to describe the many types of snow in their lives. Among them: *Za,* falling snow; *De-za,* snow that has collected on trees; *Za-he-ah-tree,* snow that the wind has blown into drifts.

That's just the start. Jerry Dennis, in his enchanting homage to atmospheric phenomena, *It's Raining Frogs and Fishes,* says there may be as many as two hundred words used by Inuit to describe snow.

De-za,
*snow that
has collected
on trees, in the
language of
Alaska's Inuit.*

De-za

SNOW PHYSICS

The physics of snow helps explain what we experience when we visit the snowy world.

Sunlight falls on the earth to begin our energy cycles, but there's a big difference in how various surfaces deal with that energy—how much of the energy is absorbed and how much reflected back into space.

When thick clouds surround Earth, they bounce back 75 to 95 percent of the solar energy. Thin clouds return 30 to 50 percent of the energy to space. Water bounces back 10 percent of the energy that strikes it. Sand reflects 15 to 45 percent, a grassy field 10 to 30 percent. Fresh snow, like the clouds from which it falls, reflects 75 to 95 percent of solar energy.

On the Trail

Finally it's time to walk on snowshoes. Happily, there's not much to it, especially if you're walking forward. Simply place one foot ahead of the other, sliding it if the binding provides free rotation, stepping if fixed. Make sure one snowshoe doesn't land on the other, or you'll tumble.

And you *will* tumble. When you fall, roll your weight onto the snowshoes, then rise. Poles help. That's the easiest recovery method, and you'll get better with practice. Try it a few times on purpose so that you'll be better able to rise when accidents happen. Jack Teegarden tells his students to untangle their legs and snowshoes, then get in the "barking dog" position, on their hands and knees, when they've fallen. "Pull one knee forward, and use that knee as a brace to help you rise," he advises.

Once you're walking, try to discover the pacing that's most comfortable for you. Space your snowshoes and steps so that you're not walking bowlegged, taking overlong steps, or stepping on your own shoes.

Backing up is a little more difficult. The easiest way to reverse direction is to make a sweeping U-turn, but that's often not possible. Stepping in reverse, it pays to watch your feet. Fixed-rotation snowshoes and free-rotation snowshoes without tails are the easiest to negotiate backward.

Snow edges carve steps in a hill.

To move across a hillside called *edging,* kick the uphill edge of the snowshoe into the hillside, to create a horizontal step. Poles will help you balance as you move.

Traversing is probably the most practical climb and descent maneuver. In this switchback edging technique, you move diagonally back and forth across the hill, creating a zigzag track up or down the hill. To make a direct ascent instead of switchback edging, kick the front of the snowshoe into the snow to create a step. Each step must be higher than the last, so that the snow doesn't collapse. Another method of ascent is the *sidestep,* in which you kick the edge of the uphill snowshoe into the snow to create a ledge you can push against to begin the next step.

If you have great traction, you can *herringbone,* turning the toes of both feet inward in a duck-like stance. Use your poles for support outside of the snowshoe steps, and make sure the traction devices of your snowshoes are firmly in place in the snow before taking each step. You can sometimes herringbone directly up even a steep hill.

Climbing is a procedure that comes with practice.

Use the edges of your snowshoes to create steps for descent. Poles help.

Going downhill may be the toughest snowshoe maneuver. The snowshoe will tend to slide, and here heel cleats are especially helpful. Keep your knees bent, leaning back a bit to place as much weight as possible on the heel cleats.

No matter which direction you're moving, try not to walk too close to rocks, trees, or shrubs, especially if they're partly covered with snow. The wind may have left snowless pockets near them, into which you might drop.

A friend, Don Chilcote of Midland, Michigan, attended college in Michigan's Upper Peninsula, where the season's snowfall is measured in hundreds of inches and snowshoes are more often a requirement than a delightful diversion. Don and a friend were walking some yards apart, hunting, when Don dropped into a hole. He'd walked over a downed treetop, which snow had covered without filling in the branches. His weight was enough to collapse the snowy ceiling, and he fell into a hole so deep that there was no sign of him on the surface of the snow. His friend walked some distance farther until he realized Don was missing. Don was still at the bottom of the hole, learning firsthand that snow effectively muffles all sound. Only with the help of his buddy did he climb back out.

USING POLES

Poles can be a great aid in helping you balance on top of your snowshoes. You can also push against poles for some forward momentum, taking some of the load off your legs and giving your upper body and arms a bit of a workout. Not least of all, poles can be used to prod the snow in search of avalanche victims. You can use cross-country or downhill ski poles, or poles made especially for snowshoeing. Some are built, in fact, to thread together and serve as avalanche poles.

Roger Addis, whose company represents the pole maker Leki, says that outfitters are encouraging people to take poles with them. "They're seeing a drop in the injury rate. You see very few creatures traveling the backcountry on two legs besides us."

Ed Kiniry of Tubbs Snowshoes recommends adjustable poles. "You can match the terrain, making the poles shorter going uphill, longer descending."

Safesport manufactures a handy tool it calls a snowpole, a single pole used the way a hiker would use a walking stick, but with a large basket to provide flotation on snow. It adds forward momentum and helps you back up, turn, rise after a fall, slow a descent, balance, and even pack snow.

Bill Prater, the Sherpa snowshoe innovator, walks with a novel combination tool: an ice ax ending in an oversize basket with a deck—a deck like a Sherpa snowshoe and bearing the company logo. He explains that the stout shaft of the ice ax lets him apply plenty of force on it if needed for a pole-style boost. The basket can be quickly removed to use the ice ax.

Poles can add balance and stability.

Bill Prater, who invented the Sherpa snowshoe, uses a custom snowshoe pole–ice ax combination.

PACKING IT IN

When heading out on the trail on snowshoes, you'll need a fanny pack, daypack, backpack, or sled to carry extra clothing, food and water, first-aid gear, and other supplies. Choose the one that best meets your needs, which may change depending on the outing.

A fanny pack, which rides at beltline and supports a small pouch, can hold a light windbreaker, a water bottle, a couple of energy bars, and a small first-aid kit—minimal gear for a quick romp in a relatively civilized setting. As you head farther out and into wilder areas, consider a daypack, a small backpack that can hold more food and water, an extra layer or two of clothing, and some additional emergency gear. A full backpack is a better bet for wilderness travel, where you should have shelter, cooking gear, a radio, and more.

A sled can serve many purposes on a trek.

A sled makes it easy to haul a heavier load, and some have been designed with winter travel such as snowshoeing in mind. Wilderness Engineering makes a sled with a cover so that a small child can ride inside. It's a good thing to have along on a trek with a small snowshoer. If your small companion tires, he or she can hitch a ride. Sleds are also good for hauling equipment and supplies, and one model by Wilderness Engineering has a pop-up tent for emergency or planned winter camping.

NAVIGATION
Using a Compass and Map
A compass and map are absolutely essential gear for the snowshoer. You can usually follow your own tracks back to civilization, but a sudden snow or a strong wind can block them out. Or you may wish to return by a different route. Learn to use a map and compass before heading out, and make sure you have them on each trip.

To use your compass independent of a map, begin by holding it level, with the direction-of-travel arrow (usually on a clear plastic base) pointed toward a landmark in the direction you've selected.

Turn the compass dial until the N on the dial lines up with the red end of the magnetic needle. The heading in degrees to your destination can be read at the index line the direction arrow provides. By pausing periodically to realign the magnetic needle and the N, your direction arrow will continue pointing the way, even if the landmark is temporarily blocked from view.

Reversing the heading, or turning the point of the direction-of-travel arrow toward you, will have you headed toward your starting point.

To use the compass with a map, first connect your location and destination points with the edge of the compass plate. Now turn the compass dial until the N on the dial points to north on the map. You can read the direction in degrees to the destination from the index line on the dial.

A topographic map offers an additional bonus for the winter traveler. By studying the closeness of the lines denoting changes in altitude, you can get a fair notion of which slopes are most likely to pose avalanche dangers—and stay well away from them.

The Global Positioning System

The *Global Positioning System (GPS),* developed in the 1970s by the U.S. Department of Defense, is another navigational aid available to the snowshoer. With GPS—and depending upon the unit you select, its format, and its ability to store waypoints and routes and compare them to map data—you can record the points along a trip for future reference, plan your next outing, avoid obstacles, or summon help to the precise point at which it's needed. GPS is used today by all branches of the military, many commercial companies, and people who travel the outdoors.

Map, compass, and Global Positioning System unit can all help you find your way on snowshoes.

PHOTO COURTESY
LOWRANCE ELECTRONICS

At the heart of the system is a constellation of twenty-four satellites, circling the earth 11,000 miles above it. Each satellite, equipped with an atomic clock, sends radio signals containing precise time information to the earth. Here, a receiver compares signals from at least three satellites to compute the receiver's precise location by triangulation. The receiver's microprocessor then translates that location onto the traditional longitude and latitude grid. From there, it compares that location, or *waypoint*, to other waypoints stored in memory.

Most units present numerical information—the distance and compass bearing to the desired waypoint. Some units can even sketch or plot the relative locations of several waypoints. Others, loaded with maps of North America or sections of it, can plot the location of the receiver relative to towns, highways, lakes, or streams.

Three satellite signals are required to compute a two-dimensional location—where on the surface of the world you are. Some units can, with a signal from a fourth satellite, also compute altitude—how far above sea level you've climbed. That's the least accurate of the readings, though.

How accurate are the GPS signals? It takes some intentional messing up to degrade them. Your government does that. There are two forms of GPS: military and civilian. Don't worry about the military one. But even the civilian signal is so accurate that through a Selective Availability (SA) program, random errors are introduced to reduce the typical accuracy of the reading from perhaps 10 yards to within 100 yards. That way, goes the military reasoning, the technology that dropped bombs down chimneys in Iraq a few years ago can't be used to drop bombs down American chimneys.

There are ways to tighten up accuracy, though. Some ground stations, their locations known accurately, receive GPS signals and compare the readings to the known location. They then broadcast the correction factor to GPS receivers equipped with Differential GPS (DGPS). Voila! You're back on the exact mark. Differential receivers are pricey, though, and not at all portable.

Most snowshoers don't need that kind of accuracy anyway, just reliable GPS units. They need to know the two ways GPS receivers can work.

Multiplexing units receive and process information from one satellite, then another, then another. If the second or third try fails, it starts at square one again. If you're moving while this goes on, you don't get an accurate location fix. If a satellite moves out of view of the receiver, sometimes because of a rock wall or thick stand of pines, the process begins all over again.

In contrast are *parallel channel* units, which receive and process the data from as many as twelve satellites at the same time, using the best three to fix location, perhaps another for altitude, and standing ready to hand off from one satellite to another as their positions change. You don't see all that happen; you just know where you are quickly and reliably.

Lowrance Electronics offers two candy-bar-size GPS parallel channel receivers, one each under the Lowrance and Eagle brands. The company advises consumers to insist on the "parallel channel" designation, since just being able to track twelve satellites, as some makers claim, doesn't mean the unit is tracking them simultaneously.

SIGNS OF LIFE

> *"The snow lay about us unmarred except for the myriads of animal tracks, some casual, some denoting a deadly purpose, others only queer little irrelevancies. I enjoyed venturing into this region of unseen life."*
> —Florence Page Jaques,
> Snowshoe Country, 1944

Winter is a good time to study the tracks and other signs of wild creatures, and it's the only season some animal signs are visible. The snowshoer leaves his or her distinctive tracks in winter's snow but also crosses the tracks and signs—and the life stories of which they tell—of many wild creatures. To read these life stories to their fullest, obtain a reliable tracking book such as Richard P. Smith's *Animal Tracks and Signs of North America*, in which much of the following introductory information was found.

Deer tracks are among those most likely to be seen by the snowshoer. Deer have two toes on each foot. When the animal is walking the toe marks may join in a shape much like an upside-down heart. Tracks of a running deer may be bunched in a foursome or may be individually spaced out in a line.

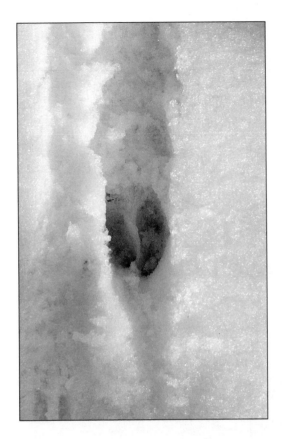

*A white-tailed
deer track.*

Moose and elk leave tracks quite a bit like a deer's, but much larger. The tracks of a running moose, in fact, may be as long as 10 inches. Elk tracks are more commonly about 4 inches long.

The tracks of most animals are much smaller and are often more difficult to distinguish. Little clues help. One good clue in track identification comes in their spacing. Squirrels, rabbits, and hares, for example, are "hoppers." Their footprints are clustered together, with blank spaces between clusters.

Squirrel tracks form a relatively rectangular shape, the four footprints fairly evenly spaced. Rabbits and hares, in contrast, leave footprints in a roughly triangular shape. The oblong hind legs are at the front of the print pattern and roughly even with each other, and the smaller front legs are behind, one of them ahead of the other. As the bunny or hare runs, its front feet land first, then the hind feet just ahead of them. Snowshoe hare tracks are much larger than those of cottontail rabbits. Hares, especially, tend to travel the same routes again and again, creating packed-down hare highways in the snow.

Members of the weasel family—weasels, mink, fishers, and pine martens—often run in such a way that they leave pairs of side-by-side depressions. This can be a little misleading, since front and back feet leave marks practically on top of one another. What may appear to be a pair of tracks may actually have been left by four weasel feet. Weasels often travel beneath the snow, too. First there are tracks in the snow, then none, then more tracks. What this means is that the critter scampered on top of the snow, then dove into it to continue its journey.

Members of the cat family, domestic and wild, are active on winter snow. Their footprints are generally circular, and unlike those of members of the dog family, their tracks do not show prints of toe-nails. Cats don't expose their toenails—their claws—until they need them. Cat track trails are quite neat, one foot hitting the snow ahead of the other, in a generally straight line. Lynx tracks are larger than those of most other cats, because they have larger feet that act as built-in snowshoes.

Tracks of members of the dog family, domestic or wild, are generally oval or oblong and usually show toenail marks in the snow. The largest of them are timber or gray wolf tracks, which can be more than 5 inches long. Groups of wolves may travel together in winter. It's tougher to tell coyote, fox, and domestic dog tracks apart.

Often in late winter or early spring, male raccoons leave their den trees to seek mates. Their snowy signatures include five toes on each foot, with the longer toes on the front footprints making them resemble human hands. When raccoons walk, their left back and right front feet land close together, as do their right back and left front.

The opossum has a distinctive track. The hind foot has a claw-less thumb, opposite the other toes.

Porcupines stay busy all winter, and their tails may leave a trail in the snow. In really deep, fluffy snow, the porky's body may even

There's other evidence of winter wildlife besides tracks.

leave a furrow in the snow. The porcupine's toes point slightly inward, and oval pads on the feet help create a distinctive track.

Muskrats spend most of their lives in and near water but sometimes strike out cross-country in winter, their rat-like tails leaving a wavy mark behind them in the snow.

Otters travel over winter's snow. More distinctive than their webbed footprints are the troughs created as their bodies plow through the snow, propelled by hind legs longer than the front ones. Small mammals are busy in winter, too. Deer mice, in particular, leave distinctive tracks that always include marks from their long tails.

Life goes on under the snow as well. Gophers, for example, burrow through the snow, lining their snow tunnels with dirt as they go.

Birds also leave evidence of their passing in the snow. Most birds have four toes on each foot, three facing forward and one

Like snowshoers, wild turkeys leave distinctive winter tracks.

backward. The rear toe is usually the shortest. Some winter birds have distinctive footprints, however. Grouse, for example, have a fourth toe that angles off to the side. Turkey tracks are 4 inches long or more, with just three toes often visible.

Beyond footprints, there are many other wildlife clues written in winter snow. Often, they tell a story of hungry animals searching for or securing winter food.

Leaves atop the snow are often an indication that a squirrel or other animal has been digging for food. Squirrels, in particular, dig down through the snow in an attempt to find acorns and other food stashed in the fall. Turkeys and white-tailed deer, among other animals, also dig through the snow in search of food.

Trees and shrubs also may show evidence of foraging activity. Rabbits and hares, deer, and some other creatures eat twigs in winter. Bunnies and snowshoes clip the twigs cleanly; deer tear them, leaving a rougher surface. Porcupines gnaw on hemlock and white cedar bark. They leave large piles of droppings, round like a deer's but longer and brown rather than black.

Beavers spend most of the winter underwater, eating food they've stashed in feed beds. But they occasionally emerge to topple new aspen trees for a fresh meal. The chips remaining from a beaver's logging job are reliable evidence, and webs can sometimes be seen in a beaver's footprints.

There's other evidence of natural drama on winter's snow. Several times I've come across the scattered feathers of a grouse that became the meal of a hawk or owl. I've seen wild turkey tracks joined by those of a coyote. In each contest, turkey wing feather tracks proved the bird detected the danger in time to fly off to safety.

Sometimes the evidence is neither of movement nor of feeding. Rabbits and hares leave *forms*, small round depressions in which they sit. The surfaces of these forms are usually iced. Deer form *beds* in the snow, oblong depressions about the size of a pillow or a little larger. Black bears spend winter in deep sleep and thus seldom leave snowy tracks. But this is a good time of the year to spot the fruit trees whose branches they broke in autumn to get at fruit and berries, or the beech trees they've marked up with their claws.

Mary Jo Griffin, walking on snowshoes, discovers evidence of a hawk or owl dining on a ruffed grouse.

Whether it's footprints, evidence of food foraging, resting spots, or lasting marks, the evidence of wildlife is seldom more accessible than it is in winter. And the snowshoer, leaving his or her own distinctive tracks across the snowy landscape, is in the best position to appreciate it.

You can help wildlife, as well as watch it, in winter. Some of this Scout crew, installing a nesting box for wood ducks, walked over the frozen marsh on snowshoes.

Snow Camping

SNOW TRENCHES

Ken Kutac's smile tells you he just flat loves winter and camping in the snow. Kutac, of White Rock, New Mexico, works at the Los Alamos National Laboratory there. But he seems to live in the snow.

I first met him on a trail heading uphill from the Solitude ski resort in Utah's Wasatch Mountains. Solitude was hosting an on-snow demonstration in which manufacturers could show retailers the latest in skis, skiwear, snowshoes, and other winter gear, then turn them loose to try out the stuff themselves. Gear makers hoped they'd come back ready to write some big orders.

When I met Kutac, he was overseeing excavation of a hole in snow more than 6 feet deep. It was to become a snow trench, one of several forms of snow shelters that, depending on the builder's situation, could serve as wonderful headquarters for a winter adventure or as a life-saving shelter from harsh elements. Kutac has used snow shelters for both.

Demo organizers, hoping to make this snow camp a little higher-tech, had erected a tent at its site. Whoever had erected this tent had lashed it to nearby trees, since it wouldn't stand on the snow on its own. A visitor asked what would happen should the area get one of the foot-deep snowfalls that often come with nightfall in the mountains.

Ken Kutac in
the entrance
of the snow
shelter in which
he camped in
Utah's Wasatch
Mountains.

"It would flat-out kill it," Kutac said somewhat contemptuously of the tent, near which he had slept the previous night—in the open, on the snow, in a bivvy sack that acted like an outer liner for the sleeping bag he had crafted himself. "I've been winter camping for thirty years, and I never sleep in a tent. I use a snow cave, a snow igloo, a snow trench, but not a tent."

He said it had been too warm the night before, sleeping in the bivvy. Too warm, but still pleasant. "Winds blew in a storm that dropped more than 15 inches overnight. It was beautiful," he said.

There are many ways to build snow shelters, Kutac said. Common to most of them is the excavation of blocks of snow from what will become the living space, and in a form that can be used to shelter that living space. Kutac favors blocks of snow 24 inches wide, 20 inches high, and 6 inches thick.

To make building blocks, he likes to begin working at a snow "face," such as the snowpack on the front of a small ridge. He trims it back with a shovel until he finds a natural surface on the snow within. Next he cuts two sides with a carpenter's saw, then carefully beneath it. Finally, he carefully cuts the back line. "The snow will drop with a *poof* when it lets go, since I created a little gap along the bottom line." With the saw still inserted in the slice at the back of the block, he pulls it away from the block to bow it slightly and coax the block out. He now has the first building block of his winter shelter.

For a snow trench, Kutac begins by carefully cutting or digging a hole just large enough to stand in, then, using the technique described above, cuts blocks from the walls within the hole. The trench should only be one block wide at the top, although it can angle out beneath the surface. Stack the blocks outside the trench and, when the under-snow excavation is completed, lean pairs of blocks against each other to cover the opening. You can cut through both of them with the saw, carefully, for a tighter face. Working down the length of the trench, you'll erect an A-frame above it. When it's complete, with an opening at one end no larger than necessary to provide entry, pile loose snow on it with a shovel, light a candle for a little light and a little radiant heat, and make yourself at home.

Kutac said that you draw oxygen from the snow itself, since up to 98 percent of the snowpack is air. "There's an unbelievable amount of oxygen in snow." The door also provides ventilation, and you can add a vent if you want to.

"Warmth and your breath will cement the structure," Kutac said. "After the first night, you can jump on the top of it and it won't break. You can put 5 feet of snow on it. I had snowmobiles run over one of them while I was inside. They're strong."

You do need to monitor weather conditions, especially in mountain areas where a storm can blow in yards of snow. Make sure your door will continue to let air in and you out. Sometimes that calls for regular shoveling.

Andy Davis excavates a snow trench (above and right), removing blocks of snow that will be used to craft an A-frame-style roof.

QUINZHEES

Instructions for a different kind of snow shelter, an Ojibwa or Chippewa structure called a *quinzhee,* were offered at an American Hiking Society Winter Trails snowshoe event.

Begin by building a mound of snow around a 7-foot pole, making the mound about 12 feet in diameter and 6 feet high in the center. Pack the snow as you pile it, then let the mound settle for about two hours.

By piling the snow up, you mixed snow of various temperatures. That set into motion water molecules that quickly freeze and bond the snow together. That's what gives the shelter its strength.

Now begin carving out an entrance hole, just large enough for your chest and shoulders. Carve directly toward the center of the mound, until you reach the pole. Then start carving equally in all directions. Small garden stakes can be used to measure the wall thickness. Kutac said he pokes sapling sticks about 8 inches long into the pile before he begins excavating; when he strikes one, he knows he's done enough digging in that direction. Formal drawings show walls 2 feet thick at the base, 1 foot thick partway up, and 10 inches thick at the top. Leave several ventilation holes.

As in the snow trench, warmth from human residents or a candle quickly seals the ceiling of the structure and strengthens it.

"The only bad thing about this structure," Kutac said, "is that you get very wet, since the snow is constantly falling on you as you dig out the inside. Waterproof clothes, and dry ones besides, are a necessity."

A quinzhee is a strong snow shelter.

Two snowshoers practice their hill skills on a quinzhee snow shelter.

At the snowshoe clinic where the AHS plans were distributed, several snowshoers testing the climbing ability of snowshoes by running up the side of the quinzhee. As two full-size men stood on top of the shelter, another visitor darted into it, unafraid.

"That's faith," said one observer.

TENTS

Many people camp in tents in winter. There are two main requirements of a tent for winter camping: that it can structurally handle the snow that may fall upon it, and that it transport water vapor from its inhabitants to the outdoors. "Four-season" tents have stouter pole systems and more rugged fabric, the better to stand against winter snow. And of course, you'll need a free-standing tent, since the ground into which you might pound tent stakes could well be buried beneath several feet of snow.

Good ventilation is important. Getting wet is the first step in getting in serious winter trouble. Often, that wetness comes not from the environment, but from the winter traveler. Remove wet clothing, and sweep out any snow that enters the tent with you. Then make sure there's adequate ventilation for water vapor from your clothing and breath to escape to the outside air before it condenses.

Use a ground cloth or tarp to keep melting snow from seeping into your shelter. Another waterproof cloth beneath your sleeping pad adds another layer of safety.

SLEEPING BAGS

Whatever shelter you select, winter camping poses special problems. Water vapor you give off may move outward through your sleeping bag, passing through insulating layers until it reaches a cool spot, where it condenses and freezes, still within the bag. On a long trip, laying out the sleeping bag each morning lets any moisture and ice turn to vapor and escape. You'll start the night with a dry bag.

Consider a sleeping bag for winter camping—a "four-season bag"—an investment. It may well cost several hundred dollars, but it will probably last a lifetime. If there's any chance of your getting wet on a winter outing, you should use a sleeping bag filled with synthetic insulation. Down, as warm and light as it is, loses most of its insulating value if it gets wet. If you're not carrying your camping gear far, you can combine two lighter bags into one or add blankets.

Some sleeping bag makers tell campers they should sleep naked to get the most insulating value from a sleeping bag. If you wish, you can stitch together a simple liner bag that can be laundered when necessary. The Campmor catalog offers flannel liners. Climbing into a sleeping bag clad in sweat-soaked clothes isn't good for the bag and is not conducive to a comfortable night's sleep.

FOOD AND WATER

Snowshoe campers, like backpackers, like to travel as light as possible. Freeze-dried foods are winners here, especially since you can boil snow for several minutes to purify it, then use it to reconstitute the food. One warning about freeze-dried foods: Manufacturers figure portions based on average meal sizes, to standards set by federal law. With all the extra energy consumed in winter activities, you're almost certain to want more than the package and the government award you. If in doubt, carry extra chow.

Fast foods, as campers use the term, are great on the snowshoe trail. High-energy bars, candy bars, mixtures of dry fruit, raisins, nuts, and candy are all good at maintaining high energy and good spirits when the body's working overtime churning out energy. Instant coffee, hot chocolate, or tea can warm your insides and brighten your disposition. Cut the amount of trash you have to carry by removing foods such as candy bars from their wrappers and boxed items from their boxes.

No camper should consider untreated water or snow safe for drinking. It should be filtered, purified, chemically treated, or boiled. Use a filter of 2 microns or smaller to avoid contracting giardiasis. Filters and purifiers used in winter must be guarded against freezing. Cold temperatures considerably extend the time it takes chemical treatments to work, and they often leave a chemical taste. Boiling makes a lot of sense, since you'll probably need to apply heat to turn snow to water anyway. Most experts say a two-minute boil kills any water-borne organisms likely to hurt you. Save some liquid water for the next boiling session to avoid burning the bottom of the pan when frying dry snow.

Keep water bottles full for drinking on the trail, remembering the higher water needs of the winter traveler. Don't let water bottles freeze, either. Kutac takes his water bottles into the sleeping bag with him when temperatures plummet. That avoids the risk of ice-plugged or even burst water bottles.

A backpacker on snowshoes has the whole wintry world as a campsite.

Campfires aren't allowed everywhere, so to be safe, take along a backpacking camp stove. In addition to liquid fuel stoves, Coleman recently launched several models of stoves that are fueled by a propane-butane blend designed to work in cold temperatures. Carry enough fuel for cooking and boiling water.

Don't use stoves inside a tent or shelter. They pump moisture into the air and remove oxygen from it. You don't want either to happen.

CAMPING MISCELLANY

Take along a few items just because they make your winter camp more homey. I hate to go anywhere without my old candle lantern, and I won't go anywhere without a journal in which I can record observations. Waterproof matches, compass, first-aid kit—all the things that help keep a camper out of trouble in the summer are doubly important in winter, when an error in judgment carries weightier penalties. Paperback book? Deck of cards? Board game? Why not? You're snowshoeing and camping for fun, after all.

8

The Happy and Healthy Snowshoer

"Perhaps no other animal suffers so much cold injury as do humans," write James Halfpenny and Roy Ozanne in their splendid book, *Winter: An Ecological Handbook.* But then, what animal spends as much voluntary, recreational time in the winter outdoors?

The snowshoer, like every winter recreationist, must be ready to deal with any adversity winter provides, avoiding as much trouble as possible by planning ahead, and dealing swiftly and skillfully with the problems that can't be avoided.

Then there comes the satisfaction of living well in a winter world that inspired Florence Jaques to write in *Snowshoe Country* in 1944: 'Thirty below,' I thought proudly, 'and this is the worst wind yet. That makes it at least sixty below, but don't tell Lee. I'm glad to report it's sixty below and rapidly getting belower.'"

COLD WEATHER BASICS

Energy from food and stored supplies powers our movements and our bodily processes and maintains our internal temperatures at about 98.6 degrees F. Our circulatory system sends blood throughout the body, carrying warmth, as well as nourishment and oxygen.

Mother Nature, though, tries to maintain an equilibrium and doesn't like one object being warmer or colder than its surroundings, so she works tirelessly to transfer our hard-earned warmth to the cold winter environment. This energy transfer happens in several ways.

Radiation is the transfer of energy through a medium without affecting the temperature of that medium. For example, sun shining through a window warms your living room without warming the glass. You lose energy to radiation through your skin.

Conduction is the transfer of energy or warmth by contact, molecule to molecule. If you touch the hood of your car in the morning, it feels cold as the warmth of your hand passes to it. Touch it after an hour in rush-hour traffic, and it feels warm as it transfers heat to your hand. You lose energy to conduction when you touch something cold.

Convection transfers energy as the medium or material surrounding the object moves. A breeze on the back of your neck creates a chill by moving the air that your neck has warmed right next to the skin. Moving water seems colder than still water. Air moving across your skin speeds your energy loss.

Evaporation transfers energy as water changes from liquid to vapor. The heat required to make this jump is taken from the water's environment—which is you if you're wearing damp clothing. You want to avoid having your energy used to evaporate water from your skin or clothes.

You also lose energy through *respiration*—warming the air you breathe. Breathing through a headband and exhaling through your mouth cuts that loss.

Comfortable temperatures can quickly become dangerous with the addition of wind. You heat the air next to your body, the wind blows that air away, and you have to start heating air again. The faster the wind blows, the more heat you need to provide the air. Eventually your body can't keep up, and you get cold. An estimate of windchill can be obtained by multiplying the wind speed by $1\frac{1}{2}$, then subtracting it from the air temperature. Thus a 20-mile-an-hour wind on a 30-degree F day presents the hazards of 0 degrees F to your body.

The snowshoer needs to guard against heat loss from each of these processes through proper shelter, insulation, windproofing, water resistance, and water avoidance.

The right clothing, the right gear, and the right snowshoes all help make for a successful outing.

KEEPING WARM

People have a lot working against them in their effort to keep warm in a wintry world. Ruth Kirk noted that we have pretty thin skin, little protective blubber (and we're constantly trying to shed it!), scant hair (and we often shave it off), and scrawny limbs that are difficult to heat efficiently. We suffer under conditions in which many other mammals thrive.

"Physiologically he is doomed," Kirk wrote of man. "Behaviorally he manages."

CLOTHING

One of the most important ways to conserve energy—and thus body heat—is to wear clothing that insulates you, keeps you dry, and keeps out the wind. A healthy, active body generally produces all the heat it needs to stay comfortable and healthy. A well-clad one preserves it. The key lies in layering—wearing well-chosen and changeable articles of clothing that perform the specialized functions of wicking moisture away from the body, insulating it, and protecting it from wind and moisture. Dressing in layers is now standard throughout the north country. With this approach, items are put on or taken off to match changing weather conditions or activity levels. They must be the right layers, though.

Snowshoers' clothing may be even more critical than that of downhill or cross-country skiers, since snowshoers often head off the trail, through the wilderness, where there's little help available if things go wrong. A snowshoer's clothing must provide insulation, breathability, and wind and water resistance.

Insulation is the ability of a material to slow or stop heat loss to conduction. Insulators such as down, wool, and synthetics such as PolarGuard and pile protect the wearer from heat loss. These materials contain dead air spaces, and air that isn't moving slows the transfer of heat and will keep your body from losing its precious warmth to the environment.

Wind-resistant clothing keeps the wind from chilling you by convection. Tightly woven or coated nylon resists wind well. Blends of nylon and cotton can also effectively shield you from both wind and water.

Water-resistant materials, such as polypropylene, shed water but will eventually soak through. *Waterproof* materials keep out all water. Some cloth has breathable waterproof membranes, with pores small enough that liquid water molecules can't get through and soak you, but your heat-generated water vapor can pass through to be carried away by the air.

Avoid *hygroscopic* fabrics, which absorb moisture from the body, the air, or the creek you fall into, and then hold it, drying very slowly. This is an invitation to a deep chill. Cotton is hygroscopic and can cause you to become dangerously chilled. "Cotton kills," says nearly every wilderness guide. Some say wet skin freezes twice as quickly as dry. Cotton provides little insulation dry, practically none wet, and it stays wet a long time, robbing the body of heat all the while. Anyone who's ever suffered a few hours in wet blue jeans knows that cotton's great for style but lousy for warmth.

Wool, made of animal hair, also holds water, but within the hairs are empty chambers that trap dead air, creating effective insulation. Wool may get wet and heavy, but it stays warm, which is why it was a favorite of smart outdoor folks long before synthetics were created. It's still popular and effective, although it's heavier than other insulators. Felt, the material of choice in boot liners, is compressed wool and will keep wet feet warm.

Wicking is the key function of the layer of clothing you wear closest to your body. In this process, water you've generated in the form of perspiration is moved away from your body and out to where it can evaporate. Both wool and polypropylene wick water. Silk is another natural fabric that wicks moisture, and it's much more comfortable against your skin than wool.

Getting Dressed

Your first layer should be quality long underwear. Outdoor folks, unless they could afford silk long underwear, once faced a choice of cotton (brrr!), wool (itchy!), or a blend. Wool still has its fans, but modern technology has developed superior synthetics such as polypropylene and polyester, which wick moisture away from the body to the next layer out. This keeps you from losing heat through conduction or evaporation.

Polyester underwear comes in three weights: lightweight, for cool weather or high activity levels, which might include snowshoeing; midweight, for a compromise most can enjoy; and expedition weight, for the coldest temperatures and limited activity such as ice fishing or hunting. Some polyesters, such as Capilene, are blended with Lycra so that they'll stretch and fit snug. Polyester works efficiently only if it is snug against the body, but it should not be so tight it restricts circulation.

Polyester can also be altered in structure, and the weaves and fiber shapes that result can help it wick more water away from your skin. Thermax, Coolmax, and Thermastat all benefit from this approach and dry quickly, insulate well, and cost more. Malden Mills alters polyester both chemically and structurally to produce Bipolar 100 (midweight) and Bipolar 200 (expedition weight) underwear, plus outerwear applications.

Your next layer should be an insulating one. Some snowshoers prefer the new lightweight fleeces, some still like wool, and others wear garments filled with down or synthetic insulation. They all work. More than one layer is best so that you can add and remove them as the temperature or your activity level rises and falls.

Over the insulating layer should be a windproof, water-resistant layer of clothing. The outer layer guards against wind and its chill—the convection effect of air moving past your body. Several new materials and treatments are available, with Gore-Tex leading the charge of proven, high-technology fabrics and treatments.

Your outfit is not complete without wool or synthetic socks, gloves or mittens that don't fit too tightly, and a hat. Ski Industries America says that 80 percent of your body's heat loss can come from radiant heat loss from the head, making hats required equipment for snowshoeing. Headbands are better than bare heads, but a full cap or hat of fleece or wool is best. If your windbreaking outer layer has a hood, better yet. Neck warmers and neoprene face masks are welcome on extremely cold days.

Gloves with breathable, waterproof membranes built into them work best. You might want both a pair of warm mittens, for the coldest days, and lighter gloves for dexterity and hand covering when the weather warms up.

You can buy socks made from the same materials as your long underwear—wool, silk, or synthetics. Again, stay away from cotton. Don't wear a sock so thick it makes your boots fit too tightly. This will restrict circulation and make your feet colder.

The following layer system is based on recommendations for skiers by Ski Industries America, which represents the makers of clothing and equipment for all kinds of winter sports. It's good advice for snowshoers, too:

- Long underwear of polypropylene or other synthetic fiber to wick away moisture from skin.
- Light shirt or turtleneck.
- Sweater of wool or fleece for insulation and warmth.
- Outer shell of windproof and water-resistant material.
- One heavyweight and one lightweight parka for changing weather conditions.
- Pair of heavy gloves and thin pair of wool, fleece, or synthetic gloves to wear under heavier ones on especially cold days.
- Headgear—headband, knitted or fleece hat, face mask—to match changing weather conditions.
- Sunblock, sunglasses and/or goggles for sunny winter days.

Keep in mind that your clothing must match both your warmest, most active moments afield and your coldest, least active ones. It must also stand ready to protect you in case of accident, wild weather changes, or other misfortune. Only by layering, and carrying extra layers, can you meet all the challenges.

Footwear

Snowshoes work with a variety of footwear. Felt pac boots are popular. They're reasonably priced and very warm, although they tend to be heavy. Mukluks such as those made by Steger Mukluks weigh half of what felt pacs do, are even warmer, and many snowshoers love them. Taiga makes boots of the same fleece that has become so popular in other winter clothing. I wore a pair of the slipper-light boots for a brisk half-hour snowshoe hike, then dallied for a half hour in 15-degree F air to chat, and never felt a chill.

Hiking boots work well for snowshoeing, especially if they're waterproof and you keep moving most of the time. Specialty snowshoers sometimes use cross-country ski or running shoes, too.

Walking in deep snow is no fun if a binding tears and you have no spare. Check bindings, especially rubber ones, for signs of wear and aging before heading out.

Boots are even being designed specifically for snowshoeing. "When snowboarding started," said Joe Guglielmetti of Tecnica, "it was with everyone wearing Sorels. Next, a dedicated shoe for snowboarding was developed. Now, it's the same with snowshoes." Tecnica, working with Tubbs, created a snowshoeing boot with a membrane that is breathable, waterproof, and stretchable. The boot is lightly insulated and features a retention strap around the ankle to keep the foot from sliding forward on descents and causing the painful affliction known as "black toe," which results from a toe slamming repeatedly into the end of a boot.

If walking on traditional, rawhide-laced snowshoes, avoid wearing boots with rugged soles, as they speed up wear of the protecting coating on the rawhide.

Gaiters are sleeves that attach to the boots to cover the boot opening and the lower part of the pants. They keep snow out of boots to help keep feet dry. Top-line gaiters made with a breathable waterproof membrane such as Gore-Tex are great, but for most uses, water-resistant material will do the trick of shedding snow, especially where the air is cold enough that snow falls off instead of clinging and melting.

COLD HAZARDS

Cold-weather woes come in two main categories: failure of the body core to maintain its heat, and cold-caused injuries to the hands and feet. The first is by far the most serious winter hazard.

The human body places the greatest importance on its core—the trunk and head—and will sacrifice hands and feet to do it. When the effort begins to fail, and the core temperature begins to fall, the human person becomes *hypothermic*.

Hypothermia

Hypothermia arrives in stages. Among other symptoms, first the skin becomes numb and shivering begins. Then the victim becomes uncoordinated and often confused. Soon he or she is stumbling, with slurred speech. Shivering stops but cooling continues, and the victim becomes incoherent. He or she becomes semiconscious, muscles rigid. Finally, the victim loses consciousness and may die.

The human body maintains an average temperature of about 98.6 degrees F; when it dips to 90 degrees F or below, we can no longer help ourselves. Often it's the relatively mild winter day that poses the greatest threat. A combination of cool temperatures, moisture, and wind sucks the warmth from a body faster than it can be produced. When that happens, nothing works right. Worst of all, the brain and its thinking process are among the first mechanisms to turn faulty.

We're lousy judges of our own thermal health. Watch your snowshoeing companions, and if they show signs of confusion or too much shivering, start treating them for hypothermia. If you suspect they're slipping toward hypothermia, they probably are. Take steps quickly.

A conscious hypothermia victim should change into warm, dry clothing; find shelter from the wind and other elements; and consume warm drinks. If the victim's core temperature drops below 90 degrees F, he or she may become incoherent or unconscious and won't be able to help him- or herself. External warming is needed. If you can summon trained medical help, do so. Experts know how to deal with the threat of continued temperature drop after rewarming. If you're the only help around, the most effective method is to share the warmth: Get into a sleeping bag with the victim, with both of you undressed. Some advise rewarming a victim in a tub of water no warmer than 108 degrees F.

Cold Injuries

Hands, feet, and facial features all have large surface areas and low volumes compared with the trunk and thus lose heat more readily. They take the brunt of cold weather and sometimes suffer frostbite.

Extremities are kept warm by blood flow from the core. If the body feels its core temperature dropping, it slows the flow to the extremities by internal constriction of blood vessels. External constriction caused by gloves, boots, socks, or even a hat that's too tight can create the same effects, and it can quickly grow serious. When hands, feet, and facial areas get too cold, they freeze.

I was taking my first dogsled ride one cold northern Minnesota morning. I thought that I, like the musher leading us, would be comfortable in fingerless wool gloves. Soon, though, I was reaching into my parka for the leather choppers that had chased away the chill on many an ice-fishing day. Holding on to the rattling sled with one hand, I pulled on a mitt, then switched to attend to the other hand. In minutes I had the choppers over the fingerless mitts, but my hands got colder. Eventually I had to stand on the sled's brake, stop the dogs, and remove both sets of hand coverings. I pulled on a single pair of looser insulated mittens musher Chris Hanson loaned me, and soon my hands began to warm back up. But it had been a close call, probably a case of frost nip. My fingertips burned for almost a week—a handicap to one who makes a living at a keyboard—but there was no deeper damage.

Frostbite is the freezing of tissue—skin and, in severe cases, the tissue beneath it. Like thermal burns, it comes in three categories:

- *Frost nip* freezes the surface of the skin, which remains flexible but white and waxy looking. Often just a warm hand or even warm breath restores it to health. It recovers much like a mild sunburn does.
- *Superficial frostbite* freezes the entire skin, but not the tissue beneath it. The skin turns red when thawed and may blister or swell. New tissue grows back, but it may take weeks to do so.
- *Deep frostbite* freezes both the skin and the tissue underneath it. The skin is white, and skin and tissue together feel hard, as if made of wood. The skin typically looks gray after it thaws. Blisters form after thawing. If the damage is severe enough, the tips of fingers, toes, or ears may blacken and fall off later.

Don't rub a frostbitten area in an effort to thaw it. Ice crystals can form between cell membranes and, when rubbed, cut through them like glass shards, making the injury worse. Don't begin treating frostbite at all if you suspect hypothermia. Frostbite threatens hands and feet, but hypothermia threatens life itself. Treat it first. Don't begin treating frostbite, either, if there's a chance the area might freeze again before help can be obtained. Refreezing will cause much greater damage.

Thawing seriously frostbitten areas is best done by experts. Remove tight clothing, wrap the affected area loosely, and seek help. If that's not possible, rewarm the area in the largest possible tub of water at 100 to 108 degrees F. Then treat it as if burned, with clean, dry dressings, elevating the injured area. Get medical help as quickly as possible. Doctors have much better tools and techniques than in even the recent past for minimizing the long-term damages of frostbite.

OTHER INJURIES

Some winter injuries are caused by the sun, especially in spring, as sunlight becomes more direct. Because snow reflects so much of the solar energy, sunburn can strike areas normally shielded. Use a sunscreen or sunblock to protect your face and other exposed areas.

Snow blindness can result from squinting at bright sun, from sunburned eyes and irises, or from sunburned retinas. Wear sunglasses or goggles with side shields, and make sure they block as many of the sun's rays as possible. Snow blindness generally heals itself with a few days of rest; still, medical care is a good idea.

Besides the special attention cold weather requires, be prepared to deal with the same kinds of lacerations, sprains, strains, and other injuries you might expect on a summer hiking trail. Carry a good basic first-aid kit, and know how to use it. (Happily, you shouldn't have to worry about the summer hazards of insects and snakes!)

MAKING HEAT

Powering your activity and maintaining your temperature both require plenty of quality fuel. It takes more food to keep a human machine running well in winter, supplied both in quick, high-energy sources such as sweets and in longer-lasting foods higher in fat. Regular fueling in smaller amounts pays the best dividends on the winter trail. Some experts recommend hourly snacks instead of, or sometimes in addition to, larger meals. Pack more food than you think you'll need. The extra load is negligible compared with the problems created if you burn more energy than you expected or the day stretches longer than planned.

The snowshoer doesn't live on food alone, either. Water's a big part of the energy equation, and though you might not seem to get as thirsty on a cold winter day as on a hot, steamy one, your need for water may be even greater. Carry plenty of water, and think of it as part of your first-aid gear—critical for avoiding injury and danger. It's not just for refreshment anymore. The extra exertion of crossing a winter landscape heats the body and frees moisture. Each breath you take must be warmed and humidified in the lungs. You expel moisture each time you exhale, maybe several extra quarts each day. Experts advise drinking a gallon of water each day. Purify all water or snow before drinking it or using it to cook (see chapter 7).

*Drink plenty
of water when
snowshoeing.*

It's fairly easy to tell if your body is dehydrated, or running low on water. Your urine output will be reduced and dark colored. Drink some water. Often, the sensations you feel as hunger are actually thirst. Drink plenty of water with meals, too.

Alcohol, incidentally, is a poor way to rehydrate. Alcohol tricks your brain into thinking you're warming up, while your body continues to cool. The combination can be life-threatening.

GOOD MANNERS AND GOOD SENSE

Most of what constitutes good manners in snowshoe country is just a matter of good sense—things like noticing the difference between ski and snowshoe tracks, realizing that what's good for one sport is poor for the other, and sticking to the trail laid for your footgear. Here are some other common sense tips:

- Bury human waste at least 1 foot deep in snow, away from trails and drainage areas. Carry out all waste paper and hygiene items.
- Camp well back from trails, developed areas, and lakes and streams.
- Carry a stove, extra clothing, and sufficient shelter if camping.
- Don't snowshoe alone in backcountry.
- Match the route and terrain to your experience, condition, and ability.
- Check weather and snow forecasts before starting your trip, and pay attention to changing conditions as you go.
- Play it smart—call off the outing if bad conditions threaten.
- If caught in a storm, make shelter and wait it out.
- Allow extra travel time when snow is soft.
- Take turns at the exhausting task of breaking trail.
- Remember that the effects of altitude are very noticeable when coupled with the vigor of a snowshoe trek, even a small one. Don't expect too much of yourself too soon.
- You'll almost always find out you've worn too much clothing, at least as long as you're moving. Make sure you have a way to carry the layers you shed.
- Be prepared for the worst possible wind, snow, and cold for the place you're heading and the season.
- Research and report any local dangers. Some wonderful snowshoe destinations in the West have *thermal areas* where hot water bubbles up through the ground. These are

Breaking trail is hard work. It's good to trade the lead frequently.

marked on maps and are sometimes bounded by fences. At Lassen Volcanic National Park in California, visitors in thermal areas, whether on foot or snowshoes, are told to stay on boardwalks. A wanderer disregarding the signs might break through the thin crust over the hot springs, plunge into scalding water, and be horribly burned or killed. An explorer named Bumpass did just that and wound up losing a leg to amputation. The thermal area into which he fell now bears the name Bumpass Hell.

- Respect water. Don't walk across lakes whose surfaces you aren't sure are safely frozen. Beware when snowshoeing near streams and rivers, too. A snowbank could give way, and swimming with snowshoes is seldom successful.

Use extra caution where local conditions, such as thermal areas, call for it.

Always plan for the worst. I asked veteran California ski patroller Frank Ward, who carries a full pack whenever he heads into the snowy backcountry, what the beginning snowshoer should carry. "Figure on spending the night," he said with a serious smile.

Ward packs a stove, fuel, water, matches and fire-starting pitch, first-aid supplies, map, high-energy food, Emergency Space Blanket or plastic tarp, a change of clothes, Gore-Tex suit, insulated plastic cup, small pan, soup, and tea. "The tarp makes a lean-to, and you can dump the stuff out of the pack and stick your feet in it and be halfway comfortable for the night." He's used almost everything he carries at one time or another.

Snow ledges along creeks may collapse if you walk on them.

SNOW-COUNTRY TRAVEL

Getting to your snowshoeing spot requires planning and common sense. Many of us travel from a land of little snow to a land of plenty. Getting there, we do well to keep in mind the suggestions of the Lassen Park Guide, prepared by the Loomis Museum Association for visitors to the Northern California park, whose roads vanish under deep snow and whose trails draw skiers and snowshoers each winter.

- Carry tire chains.
- Be alert for icy roads and drifting snow.
- Slow down when daylight and weather conditions change.
- Watch out for other drivers; drive defensively.
- Beware of snowplows; slow down slowly, and keep to the right on curves.
- Stay well back from snowplows and other heavy equipment.
- Stay on plowed roads.

To avoid all kinds of cold-related injuries and snowshoeing problems, remember that you need to keep generating heat and to retain it. Eat often. Use activity to warm up and rests to cool off. Avoid becoming exhausted. Pace the outing to the comfort level of the least conditioned of the group. And leave the snowy landscape the way you'd like to find it next time. That way everybody stays warm, healthy, and happy.

9

Avalanche

Frank Ward stopped and reached into a snowbank. "There's a pretty good layer of ice, with 10 inches of snow on top of it. If we get some more snow, it could be trouble." Gazing at the Northern California hillside within Lassen Volcanic National Park, he pointed to some large rocks and trees. "There are enough ground anchors to hold the snow. When the snow gets deep enough to be smooth, with no anchors showing, I watch it even more."

Trained ski patroller Frank Ward reaches into the snowpack and extracts a sample. The slick-packing snow is one sign that conditions may be building toward danger on some slopes.

*Ski patroller
Frank Ward*

Ward, a member of the National Ski Patrol, who often visits this park and others—sometimes to help rescue snowshoers or skiers in trouble—was explaining some of the dynamics of avalanche to this flatlander from Michigan.

"Nothing in nature outdoes new-fallen snow as a symbol of peace and purity," Ruth Kirk writes in her book *Snow.* "And nothing holds quite the same Jekyll-and-Hyde capacity to turn serenity into chaos." She was speaking of avalanche.

Avalanche is the fearsome downhill slide that can level homes, topple trees, and bury winter sports enthusiasts beneath the snow they've come to love. Unrescued, they slowly suffocate under the snow. Half of them interred for thirty minutes die.

When conditions threaten, resorts in avalanche areas often lock skiers into lodges, allowing no one to come or go until the danger has passed. It's not unheard of for visitors to spend several days stranded at popular resorts, where food and space can run scarce. Roads into Utah's Wasatch Mountains are often closed when avalanche dangers rise, reports of which are as common as in-town traffic congestion reports on radio stations in Salt Lake City. One expert told the *Salt Lake Tribune* in a 1997 interview that 98 percent of avalanche accidents come in slides the recreationist himself or herself causes, not in controlled ski areas or on highways. They come when skiers, snowmobilers, and snowshoers set them off.

It's probably impossible to completely avoid the danger of avalanche when visiting mountainous country. It is very possible, though, to lessen your risk of being buried by an avalanche, and to boost the odds that you or a member of your party will survive one.

If you're going to be snowshoeing in avalanche country, you need additional training. What follows is only introductory information. Get the specifics from an avalanche expert or one of the many good avalanche schools conducted throughout mountainous regions.

AVALANCHE FACTS

There are two types of avalanches, *loose snow avalanches*, which begin at a single point on a slope and become wider and wider as they flow downhill, and *slab avalanches*, which begin at a fracture line, a place where the surface of the snow is broken. In it, a large area of snow begins to flow at once, often when a weak layer of snow such as depth hoar breaks loose.

Several factors go into avalanche prediction and avoidance, including snow type, snowfall, slope, and air temperature.

Within the two avalanche categories, avalanches can be made of wet snow, as is often the case in spring, or dry, the kind of cold-weather snow that creates the swiftest avalanche. It depends on the type of snow on the ground. Of the various types of snow crystals, stellar crystals and dendrites tend to lead to stable snowpacks. Graupel, needles, pellets, and mixed snows tend to spell trouble.

Though it would seem logical that well-packed snow would present little hazard to the winter traveler, that's not the case. Tightly packed snow often forms slab avalanches. That's why veterans of avalanche country travel dig snow pits and reach into drifts to inspect for layers. When a foot of snow stands poised on an icy layer and a slope leads it downhill, it may break loose and head in that direction. You don't want to be in its path.

Guard against a wet-snow avalanche by paying attention to the moisture content of the snow. Danger increases when the moisture content reaches and surpasses 10 percent—about the level at which you can pack a decent snowball that feels a little slippery in your hand.

Most avalanches occur during or just after a storm. Danger rises when new snowfall reaches 12 inches or more. Avalanche danger increases anytime snowfall reaches a rate of 1 inch per hour or more, as the snow doesn't have time to stabilize. Some say 1/2 inch per hour spells danger, as does 1/4 inch with wind. High winds make leeward slopes—those downwind or on the back side of a peak—especially dangerous, even if the snow cover is relatively light.

Logic might seem to dictate that the steepest slopes would pose the highest avalanche risks, but that's not the case. Those sharp hillsides, like the steep-pitched roofs of homes in snow country, shed their loads of snow long before they build much depth.

It's the midrange slopes, those of 30 to 60 degrees, that collect layer after layer of snow, sometimes shedding them all at once in a thundering slide that can spell death to those below. Slopes of 30 to 45 degrees are the most dangerous of all. Slopes that are convex, bulging out from the hillside, are more dangerous than those that are concave, bowing into it. The air temperature can affect avalanche danger. Snow tends to stabilize at about the freezing point. Colder temperatures lead to the formation of depth hoar, a layer of unstable snow, which encourages avalanche. Warmer air tends to make snow heavier and more prone to slide.

North-facing slopes are the most dangerous, especially in deep winter, as they have the coldest air, and dramatic temperature differences between the ground and air encourage the development of depth hoar. Come spring and on sunny days, however, south-facing slopes draw more solar energy, which could raise the risk of a wet avalanche. In all seasons, downwind sides of hills pose higher danger, since their snow is deeper and often in layers of slabs.

There are clues to avalanche-prone areas. A lack of trees is a good one. Chances are that a bald spot was created by a previous avalanche, and the same areas tend to host avalanches time after time. Freshly downed trees, all pointing in the same direction, may have been laid down by avalanche. A V-shaped, treeless gully may have been trimmed by sliding snow.

The following are some precautions when snowshoeing in avalanche country:

- Weather that's changing rapidly can make snow unstable. Fast changes in wind, temperature, or snow cover can mean trouble.
- If you hear a strange sound underfoot, one sometimes described as "whumff," that can be a signal of unstable snow—and a sign you're in dangerous terrain.
- If you see signs of a recent avalanche, be careful of another. If you see broken trees, old slide paths, and similar evidence of past slides, figure you're in a slide-prone area.
- If you have no choice but to cross what appears to be a dangerous slope, pick a path near the top. Stay away from any obvious fracture lines.
- If you have no choice but to climb or descend a dangerous slope, go straight up or down it.
- Open slopes can be trouble. Dense tree growth, ridges, or rocky outcrops provide some cover and act as anchors for the snow.

- "Only one person should cross a dangerous slope at a time," advises the Lassen Volcanic National Park visitor guide. "Put on hat and mittens and fasten clothing securely. Carry and use an avalanche beacon."

COPING WITH AVALANCHE

When an avalanche breaks loose, watch every detail, especially if you see someone swept away. If you're left standing after an avalanche but others are buried in the snow, mark the place where you last saw them. Then begin searching directly downhill of that mark.

Paths bulldozed by avalanches in the past (above and right) are likely spots for a repeat occurrence.

Move across the snow, poking into it with avalanche poles, ski poles, a shovel, or a ski. If possible, send someone for help. Many backcountry travelers carry radios or cell phones so that they can summon help in an emergency. In this case, you have an extra rescuer instead of a courier, and the message is delivered much quicker.

Keep looking. The person trapped in the snow has less than a 50 percent chance of survival after thirty minutes, but even long odds are worth the effort if you pull a revivable victim from the snow. And miracles do happen.

If you're the victim, try to stay on your feet while tossing aside all the gear you can. Get out of your snowshoes, if possible. Try to swim in the snow. After all, it's just colder, thicker water. Try to work your way to the edge of the avalanche flow. As the slide stops, work to create some space around your face, and cover your face with a hand. Spit to determine which way is down, and then try to poke one hand to the surface.

Seasoned snow patroller Frank Ward, a member of the National Ski Patrol, carries a daypack in which he always keeps a radio, a full Gore-Tex suit, food, stove, water, fuel, rope for rescue, first-aid gear, map, avalanche shovel, and more. Frank's ski poles are threaded to lock together as an avalanche pole that can be poked into the snow to locate buried skiers or snowshoers. Locating the victim is only the first step in saving that avalanche victim. Then comes the task of digging him or her out. Most victims are buried under 5 feet of snow. Frank carries an avalanche shovel whose handle extends, for better digging.

Some mountain travelers carry avalanche cords, lightweight, visible ropes that tend to float on top of sliding snow. If a traveler lets the rope trail and is then caught in an avalanche, the rope may lead a rescuer to the victim.

Avalanche country visitors also often carry avalanche beacons, small radio transmitter-receivers that can guide help to a victim's burial site. Rescue beacons are set to transmit when the outing begins. If someone is lost, others in the party turn off their transmitters (conditions permitting) and use their receivers to lead them to the victim. Not all avalanche beacons are compatible; in order for the technology to protect your party, all beacons must be on the same frequency.

The unit is used in one straight line, back and forth, to find the strongest signal. The rescuer then turns 90 degrees and moves back and forth along the other horizontal axis, with the receiver's power dialed down to make it easier to hear fine differences and find the strongest signal in that direction. Where the lines intersect, the rescuer should be standing right over the victim.

Running and Racing

One reason to don snowshoes is to enjoy the wonderful winter world outside. Another good one is to improve the world inside you.

Snowshoeing—brisk but regular walking on snowshoes—can burn about 9 calories per minute, 500 calories or more per hour. Walking at a moderate pace burns calories at about half that rate. Raise the intensity level of your snowshoeing activity, and you boost the energy consumption.

"Snowshoeing in deep snow," says the *Berkeley Wellness Letter*, "can provide nearly as good a cardiovascular workout as stair-climbing. If you use ski poles when you walk, that adds an upper-body workout."

And many do set their sites aerobically higher. Ski Industries America, an industry group that also represents snowshoe and snowboard makers, says that three distinct groups of snowshoers have emerged: those who climb mountains, those who meander through the snowy world, and those who run, race, and pursue fitness on snowshoes. Many in the third category come to snowshoeing from similar summertime activities.

RUNNING SNOWSHOES

Snowshoe runners will find a healthy market of running snowshoes awaiting them. Redfeather's first snowshoes were designed for running. Sherpa's Bolt and Tubbs's 10K are running specialists. YubaShoes has several running models, as do other companies.

*Running
snowshoer.*

"Running snowshoes are gaining in popularity," says Ski Industries America. "Many companies make the special [snow] shoes built for cross training or fitness running on hard-packed, snowy trails. Running snowshoes tend to be smaller—about 8 inches wide and 25 inches long—and narrower than trekking shoes, and they are extremely lightweight, compared to their cousins which are used in deep snow. Regular running shoes are generally worn with the running snowshoes, but light hiking boots can also be used."

Snowshoe racing, shown here and on pg. 124, has become a popular pursuit all its own.

SNOWSHOE RACING

Running on snowshoes invariably led to racing on snowshoes, and you can now enter events as strenuous as you'd like. Snowshoe races commonly range from 5 kilometers to more than 100 miles.

Snowshoe running and racing are gaining in popularity, as is just about everything else about this sport. In 1987 there were about a dozen snowshoe races in the United States; by 1994 there were more than fifty; a few years later, there were hundreds at all levels. *Time* magazine reported in 1991 that the U.S. Snowshoe Association was lobbying to get snowshoe racing accepted as an Olympic event.

Organizers of a community winter festival in Grayling, Michigan, included a snowshoe race on their calendar. They started with a 1-mile race—three laps on a groomed trail that circled the recreation area softball field, with a couple of passes through woodlots. Then, to spice it up, make it into something of a biathlon, and nod to the area's fame as the birthplace of Fred Bear's pioneering Bear Archery Company, they added a stop on each of three laps at which racers picked up a bow and shot three arrows at a large target. Misses brought reductions in time and finishes.

In this mock biathlon, snowshoe racers stopped on each lap to shoot arrows at a target.

Other races offer different kinds of challenges. Some mix cross-country skiing and kayaking into the competition. One of the toughest of the racing contests is the Lake Superior Challenge snowshoe race, held each winter in northern Minnesota. The race covers 76 miles in four days. There's no trail; competitors must orienteer, camp out, and deal with anything nature throws at them.

Sherpa, like many makers, builds asymmetric snowshoes just for racing, which until recently was done on packed trails. "Out in Colorado, though," said Sherpa staffer Jeff Sipola, "they decided that was too boring. Now they race in powder," a setting that is far more strenuous since the snowshoes sink into the fluff, and some races mix both trails and powder. Sherpa is fine-tuning a design for a snowshoe that will excel on runners' and racers' feet in both kinds of snow.

Racing starts with running. New snowshoe runners should try their normal gait first. If the tail of the shoe strikes the snow first, try switching to running on the balls of the feet, then flexing the toe toward the shin to raise the snowshoe from the snow.

Fitness fans don't need groomed trails. This snowshoer is running through a snow-filled swamp.

Who's Who in Snowshoes

The snowshoe industry is a thriving one. More than twenty companies make snowshoes in a wide range of designs, materials, and prices. Model names and offerings change from year to year, but what follows is a general guide to who makes what. Write to individual companies or check with local specialty shops for up-to-the-minute details.

SNOWSHOES

> Atlas Snow-Shoe Company
> 1830 Harrison St.
> San Francisco, CA 94103
> phone: 800-645-SHOE
> fax: 415-252-0354
> www.atlasworld.com

Atlas has four series of snowshoes. The Summit Series is made for climbing, backcountry travel, snowboarding, and skiing in extreme terrain. The Hiking Series is for day hikes and for winter camping in any terrain. The Atlas Walking Series is for winter casual hiking in rolling or flat areas. And the Running Series is for trail running on packed or firm snow. All feature Atlas's patented rear heel cleat and spring-loaded binding. Atlas's T.I.G. welded seams are patented, as is the spring-loaded binding that lifts the nose of the snowshoe with each step.

Baldas Snowshoes
Vanguard Development International
1660 17th St., Suite 110
Denver, CO 80202
phone: 303-607-9498

Baldas snowshoes are made in France, where they are tested and proven in the Alps. They are lightweight, with sport models at 2.6 pounds per pair and backcountry models at 3.5 to 3.7 pounds. They feature maximum support with minimum surface area and have simple binding systems. Models are available in polypropylene or nylon web decking.

Glacier Snow Shoe Company
Strikemaster Corporation
17217 Highway 10 East
Big Lake, MN 55309
phone: 612-263-8999
fax: 612-263-8986

Glacier makes two models, both of seamless 6063T52 extruded high-strength aluminum tubing. Decks are made of a PUC blend–polyester material, with a highly abrasion-resistant coating. All come with factory-installed bindings and a two-year warranty against defects in materials and manufacturing. The Yetna, 9 by 24 inches, is designed for a load of up to 200 pounds. The Kahilta, at 9 by 34 inches, is for loads of 200 pounds and more.

Good Thunder
3945 Aldrich Ave. South
Minneapolis, MN 55409-1413
phone: 612-824-2385

Good Thunder has a range of snowshoes, from its UltraLight Racer at 26 ounces per pair to the 10-by-42-inch Alaska Trekker. The company says its BioLogic frame blends maximum flotation, anatomical correctness, and articulating, aggressive crampons in its Technical/Performance Series. Good Thunder's Winterrific Series includes a kid's snowshoe, a hiking and running snowshoe, and a backcountry hiking and recreational snowshoe.

> G & V Snowshoes (Raquettes G & V Engineering)
> P.O. Box 87
> Loretteville, Quebec, Canada G2B 3W6
> phone: 418-842-0321
> fax: 418-842-2003

G & V makes a full line of traditional and modern snowshoes. The Snow Trail has an aluminum frame plus a patented tubular connector bar for maximum pivot and lateral control. The decking is made of Olafin thermoplastic. The Winter Trail recreational snow-shoe has many of the same features. G & V Wild Trail snowshoes are for serious runners. The Mountain Trail folds up for transport in backpack, car, or snowmobile. The company also makes an adjustable fiberglass Snowshoe Pole. Traditional snowshoes by G & V include the Huron Type, for use on trails or in open wood-lands; the Modify Bear Paw, for emergency or snowmobile excur-sions; the Bear Paw, for dense woods; the Alaskan, for open ground and deep snow; the Ojibwe, for sliding travel in open country with deep snow; and the Montagnais and Cod types, both oval shaped for use in forest and deep snow. Many of these models are avail-able with neoprene lacing, in addition to traditional rawhide. Spe-cial nylon-laced snowshoes are designed by G & V for strength and light weight. Special heavy-duty models are hand-woven with polypropylene rope. G & V also makes a no-maintenance polyethyl-ene snowshoe and several types of bindings.

Iverson Snowshoe Co.
Box 85
Maple St.
Shingleton, MI 49884
phone: 906-452-6370
fax: 906-452-6480

Iverson makes snowshoes with traditional wooden frames of veneer-quality white ash, lacing them with either traditional rawhide or nylon-reinforced neoprene, which, it says, "has proven immune to all of rawhide's shortcomings and is formulated to withstand a lifetime of recreational use."

The Iverson line includes Cross Country, Green Mountain modifications of the bear paw, Michigan, double-pointed Ojibwa, Alaskan Trail, Youth for kids from toddler to lightweight teen size, and a popular Westover modification of the bear paw pattern. Iverson also offers Modified H neoprene and A-style nitrile-coated polyester bindings, the Bob Maki Sno-Paws rubber binding, and Gregory Crampons, which fit all wooden-framed, laced snowshoes.

Little Bear Snowshoes
Spring Brook Manufacturing, Inc.
2477 I Rd.
Grand Junction, CO 81505
phone: 970-241-8546
www.springbrook.com/snowshoe

Little Bears are designed as entry-level, first snowshoes. Key features include a binding system that adapts to almost any style or size of footwear, and a toe-forward placement of the foot on the platform, which does not have a toehole. You basically walk on a large sole that's an extension of your foot pointing straight forward. Wearers can climb slopes of 45 degrees. Since the entire platform lifts off the snow, walking backward or through heavy cover is made simpler. They're small, just 11 by 17 $\frac{1}{2}$ inches, yet will support more than 200 pounds under most snow conditions. They weigh about a pound each. Stainless steel studs improve traction, and predrilled holes allow snowboard or cross-country ski bindings to be attached.

Spring Brook also makes Little Bear Cubs, 6-by-14-inch snowshoes designed for kids. They feature the Kinder Binding, a junior ski binding that can be set at three different adjustment positions to match the foot of the wearer.

> MSR
> Mountain Safety Research
> P.O. Box 24547
> Seattle, WA 98124
> phone: 800-877-9677
> fax: 206-224-6492

MSR's Denali Llama snowshoes are 22 inches long in their basic incarnation. The lightweight, one-piece platforms of polypropylene support a lace and hook binding, a crampon, and MSR Traction Bars, whose toothed steel rails provide extra grip, especially on ice or side slopes. For more flotation, you can add long or short flotation tails, creating a snowshoe 26 or 30 inches long.

> Powder Wings
> Wing Enterprises
> 1325 W. Industrial Circle, P.O. Box 3100
> Springville, UT 84663-3100
> phone: 801-489-3684
> fax: 801-489-3685
> www.powderwings.com

Powder Wings manufactures neoprene-decked snowshoes with shock-corded anodized aluminum frames, made of Easton 7075 aluminum alloy, that are assembled much like backpacking tent frame poles. Unassembled, the snowshoes fit in a fanny pack. Assembled, they're 9 by 28 inches, with adjustable bindings, for snowshoers weighing up to 220 pounds. Other models are available in larger and smaller sizes.

Redfeather's Penguin is a take-down snowshoe at an entry-level price.

Redfeather Snowshoes
4955-D Peoria St.
Denver, CO 80239
phone: 800-525-0081
fax: 303-375-0357
www.redfeather.com

Redfeather offers three series of snowshoes to match conditions and uses. The Arc-Tech Series features inexpensive, two-piece, light-weight polymer snowshoes that collapse and reassemble quickly. The Leadville Series is a high-tech, high-performance line, with a

Control-Trak II binding. This is Redfeather's top of the line and includes the company's original offerings. The Redfeather Sport Series, like the Leadville Series, has Zemid tailplugs to protect the short tail-style ending. These snowshoes are built on polished aluminum frames, with new molded bindings.

Redfeather accessories include a Polar Heel Lift, titanium front talon, snowboard boot binding, insulated spats, and insulated toe cover. The company also offers probe poles, telescoping poles, carry bags, snowboard packs, and other snowshoeing accessories.

Safesport Manufacturing Co.
269 Columbia Ave.
Chapin, SC 29036
phone: 800-433-6506
fax: 803-932-4610

Safesport makes traditional snowshoes and hybrids, as well as some more modern styles. Safesport's premium Northwoods snowshoe line is made with New England hardwood frames, laced by hand with full rawhide or durable neoprene, and double varnished. Safesport's Freetrail line has wood frames decked with solid neoprene that is perforated so snow won't cling. The deck is reinforced by eyelets and tightened inside the frame by nylon-covered cable. The binding is attached with screws and nuts in a pivot system.

The Winter Hiker Series are economical snowshoes with high flotation. They feature green deckings made of copolymer, with spikes on the bottom side and a nonslip heel section on the top, and neoprene bindings. The SnowTrek line from Safesport is an economy line laced with split rawhide and designed for the amateur who wants a limited-duty snowshoe.

Safesport also manufactures a heavy-duty thermo-plastic Michigan-style snowshoe it says is ideal for beginners, rugged terrain, and no-maintenance ownership. The company also offers a rawhide repair kit for snowshoes and several types of crampons and bindings, including cross-country, Salomon Nordic system, sandal-style, A-style, H-style, rubber, and latex bindings.

Sherpa Snowshoes
444 S. Pine St.
Burlington, WI 53105
phone: 800-621-2277
fax: 414-763-4506

Sherpa makes snowshoes in three general categories: hiking, backpacking, and mountaineering snowshoes for high-performance applications; recreational hiking and walking snowshoes for packed or broken trails; and jogging and running snowshoes. There are several lines within these categories.

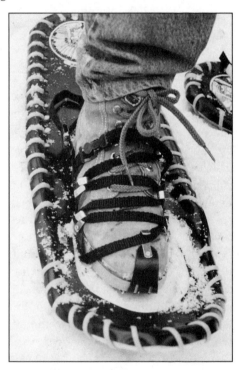

Sherpa's popular Sherp-Fit binding on its economically priced Indian Summer snowshoe.

The Tech line brings Sherpa innovations to market. The Mountain line of snowshoes offers tried and proven performance and features deck-securing lacing in numerous compartments. Should a lace be broken by accident on the trail, although that's unlikely given the thick, tough material, the rest of the snowshoe will remain laced and the wearer can snowshoe on. Bolt snowshoes are designed for the special needs of the snowshoe runner and aerobics athlete. And the Indian Summer line provides solid snowshoe value at a lower price.

In addition to its long-popular, flexible Sherp-Fit binding, Sherpa now offers a Bill Prater Step-In binding for use with Black Diamond crampon-compatible mountaineering boots.

> TSL Snowshoes
> 925 N.W. 19th, Suite A
> Portland, OR 97209
> phone: 503-241-9380

TSL is a French firm that offers several styles of polypropylene snowshoes, from a high-tech model to one for children. All feature steel spikes for extra grip. TSL bindings come in several configurations, from simple rubber slip-ons to bindings for hiking boots and cross-country ski boots.

> Tubbs Snowshoe Company
> 52 River Rd.
> P.O. Box 207
> Stowe, VT 05672-0207
> phone: 800-882-2748
> fax: 802-253-9982

Tubbs offers several lines of snowshoes. The Expedition Series includes three models for hiking, backpacking, and mountaineering; they feature anodized aluminum frames, Quadex decking, and an RCS binding system, which holds the heel of the hiking boot snugly for precise tracking and sidehill traverses. The Altitude Series is designed for hiking, backpacking, or backcountry snowboarding in variable powder or packed powder. Snowshoes in this line feature aluminum frames, Quadex decking, and TD91 bindings, with Control

Wings and rigid bases. The Adventure Series is made for day hikers and sport walkers. These snowshoes have decks made of a combination of Quadex and Hypalon and TDS bindings, with Control Wings and rigid bases.

The Traditional Series includes the Green Mountain Bear Paw, with a handcrafted select northern white ash frame, top grain rawhide or neoprene lacing, and TD91 Control Wing binding. The Trekker Series has an aluminum frame inserted into a one-piece molded polyurethane decking. The Just for Kids Series is for young snowshoers. The Aerobic Series offers a lightweight, asymmetrically shaped snowshoe for winter runners, multisport athletes, and aerobics enthusiasts. The 10K is a model worn by many veteran snowshoe racers and runners.

Tubbs also offers accessories, including Nordic and snowboard binding plates, bindings, crampons, and lacing kits.

> Ursus Snowshoes
> 2019 E. 7th Ave.
> Vancouver, British Columbia, Canada V5N 1S5
> phone: 604-254-4517
> fax: 604-254-6604
> e-mail: alpinist@freenet.vancouver.bc.ca

Ursus specializes in snowshoes made with the latest high-tech metals and composites, including 6061-T6 seamless drawn aluminum alloy, nylon-core DuPont Hypalon decking, and stainless steel crampon points. It offers standard and step-in bindings, and accessories including ice axes and poles.

> Wilcox & Williams
> phone: 800-216-0710
> www.snowshoe.com

Wilcox & Williams offers kits and finished Ojibwa, Alaskan, bear paw, and kids' model snowshoes, plus bindings, equipment, books, and even snowshoe furniture.

Winterstick Snowboards
435 W. 200 S., Suite 201
Salt Lake City, UT 84101
phone: 801-521-5010
fax: 801-521-6217

Winterstick's Vert snowshoes, ultralight injection-molded snow-shoes, are made for climbing in soft snow and powder. The 2 1/2-pound-per-pair snowshoes fit into any daypack and have a scalloped toe design and a crampon-style base. They're made for climbing straight uphill, without the effort of zigzag climbing and traversing, and are especially for snowboard enthusiasts eager to climb a hill and then snowboard back down it.

YubaShoes Sport Snowshoes
1157 W. Sunset Blvd.
Rockin, CA 95765
phone: 800-598-YUBA

Yuba Sport Snowshoes feature asymmetrical frames, rather than the standard symmetrical designs of traditional and most modern snowshoes. "Our frames look different because they are designed like the natural shape of your foot," says a company brochure, "the stable platform that Mother Nature gave you."

Yuba shoes feature a slotted platform binding and front and rear cleat systems. Models include cross-training and racing snowshoes, walking and recreational snowshoes, backcountry snowshoes, and models for kids ages four through twelve. Bindings are avail-able for running snowshoers, cross-country boot wearers, and those snowshoeing in climbing and telemark boots, as well as standard bindings for all kinds of winter footwear.

Yuba's Summit Series features the Yuba Heel Lift, a wire bail that levers forward to hold the heel above the snowshoe base to make climbing easier. The Borderline Series features entry-level snowshoes. The Sport Line and Leadville series are designed for hiking, backpacking, and mountaineering.

SNOWSHOE ACCESSORIES

One snowshoe maker says all you need to buy is snowshoes; you already own everything else you need. Still, many items make snowshoeing more efficient, safer, or more enjoyable. What follows is only a sampler of the accessories available.

> Leki-Sport USA
> 60 Earhart Dr.
> Williamsville, NY 14221
> phone: 800-255-9982
> fax: 716-633-8063

Leki poles work as well for snowshoeing as for skiing, adding balance and security while boosting the snowshoer's endurance. Leki Trekking poles are made with 7075 aluminum alloy shafts. Adjustment is made through an Expander Adjustment System, using a plastic dowel that is always in contact with the inside walls of the next larger shaft. The dowel expands to lock the shafts in place. Baskets are interchangeable to match snow conditions.

Leki poles lend balance and power to snowshoers, here moving on modern snowshoes.

PHOTO COURTESY LEKI-SPORT USA

Steger Mukluks
125 N. Central Ave.
Ely, MN 55731
phone: 218-365-6634
fax: 218-365-5329

Steger manufactures the traditional cold-weather footgear that offers lightweight warmth. Favored by many on extreme expeditions, the mukluk is loved by many snowshoers, too.

Survival on Snow, Inc.
Box 1, Site 218, RR #2
St. Albert, Alberta, Canada T8N 1M9
phone: 403-973-5412
fax: 403-973-3318

Survival on Snow (SOS) makes avalanche shovels, avalanche probes, and the SOS F1-ND Avalanche Beacon, a 457 kHz unit that features a 90-meter range; built-in safety checks; automatically forced-on switch; built-in battery, receive, and transmit checks; and separate chest and neck straps.

Taiga
1160 Labrant
P.O. Box 2227
Bigfork, MT 59911
phone: 406-837-0177
fax: 406-837-2309

Taiga says that its superlight boots are a perfect match for modern, superlight snowshoes. Taiga boots weigh just 1 warm pound. They're made with Polartec 200 Double Water Repellency fleece, with adjustable ankle strap, independently adjustable toe strap, and heat-trapping, open-cell polyurethane footbed. Waterproofing materials, the company says, are thermal conductors and rob the feet of heat while protecting them from water. So Taiga uses fleece to keep the heat in, wet or dry.

Tecnica USA
19 Technology Dr.
West Lebanon, NH 03764
phone: 800-258-3897
fax: 603-298-5790

Tecnica, working with the Tubbs Snowshoe Company, developed the Snow Paw, a lightweight (2 pounds, 8 ounces per pair) snowshoe-specific boot with a removable instep pressure distribution system, adjustable heel retention strap, special insulation, and Tecni-Dry waterproof-breathable system.

The Tecnica Snow Paw boot, designed by Tecnica and the Tubbs Snowshoe Company.

PHOTO COURTESY
TECNICA

The SNOWSHOER
COMM-STRAT Publishing
P.O. Box 458
Washburn, WI 54891
phone: 715-373-5556
fax: 715-373-5003
e-mail: JimCampRV@aol.com

The Snowshoer, published five times a year, is dedicated to the world of walking on snow. In articles and advertising, it is a solid and up-to-date reference on new developments in snowshoeing.

Wilderness Engineering
214 W. 1000 S.
Ogden, UT 84404
phone & fax: 801-399-4096

Wilderness Engineering's Base Camp Sled System features rotationally molded, cross-linked plastic hulls, for durable, flexible, stable sleds. Poles are made of chrome moly steel, stronger than aircraft aluminum, and are powder coat finished. Sleds come with removable duffel bags and a fully adjustable harness system that can be fitted to almost any waist for hands-free snowshoeing, even while lugging a large load on the sled.

The KinderShuttle is a sled system designed for pulling kids on backcountry ski trails. Hull, harness, and poles are the same as for the Base Camp, but a DuPont Cordura canopy and clear vinyl windscreen have been added to protect youngsters while allowing them to enjoy the wintry outdoors.

Special Mention

Carl Heilman
R.R. 1, Box 213A
Brant Lake, NY 12815-9743
phone: 518-494-3072

Heilman manufactures custom snowshoes and, as a New York licensed guide, also leads snowshoe tours. He also has a snowshoe book in the works.

Jack Teegarden, Maker
17999 Hunter's Home Rd.
Atlanta, MI 49709
phone: 517-785-2459

Jack Teegarden no longer makes custom snowshoes for sale, but he still refurbishes and refinishes keepsake and heirloom snowshoes and teaches snowshoe building and snowshoeing.

MAIL-ORDER SUPPLIERS
Several catalogs offer snowshoes and snowshoeing gear. The following are some of my favorites.

> The Boundary Waters Catalog
> Piragis
> 105 N. Central Ave.
> Ely, MN 55731
> phone: 800-223-6565

Snowshoes, books, equipment.

> Cabela's
> 812 13th Ave.
> Sidney, NE 69160
> phone: 800-237-4444

Snowshoes, including own brand, outdoor gear.

> Campmor
> P.O. Box 700-Q
> Saddle River, NJ 07458-0700
> phone: 800-230-2151

Snowshoes, poles, gaiters, clothing, avalanche shovel.

> Early Winters
> P.O. Box 4333
> Portland, OR 97208-4333
> phone: 800-458-4438

High-tech underwear, insulating layers, outerwear, sunglasses,
avalanche beacon.

REI
(Recreational Equipment Inc.)
1700 45th St. East
Sumner, WA 98390

Snowshoes, poles, full range of outdoor gear.

References

Acerrano, Anthony. "Frostbite: The Cold Reality." *Sports Afield* (February 1996): 40.

American Hiking Society. "Choosing the Shoe That's Right for You." News release, 1997.

Atwill, Lionel. "Staying on Top (Hunting in the Big Chill)." *Field & Stream* (December 1994): 46.

Backpacker's Pantry. *1997 Retail Catalog*.

Berman, Bob. *Secrets of the Night Sky: The Most Amazing Things in the Universe You Can See with the Naked Eye*. New York: William Morrow and Company, 1995.

Cohoon, Sharon. "Snowshoeing Takes a Leap!" *Outdoor Retailer* (March 1989).

Danziger, Lucy S. "Snowshoe Chic." *Vogue* (December 1995).

Dennis, Jerry. *It's Raining Frogs and Fishes: Four Seasons of Natural Phenomena and Oddities of the Sky*. Drawings by Glenn Wolff. New York: HarperCollins Publishers, 1992.

Densmore, Frances. *Chippewa Customs*. St. Paul: Minnesota Historical Society Press, 1929, 1979.

Eastern Mountain Sports. *Cold Weather Layering*. Brochure, 1995.

Finkel, Michael. "Red-Hot in the Snow." *Sports Illustrated* (December 12, 1994).

Foley, Dave. "New Look in Snowshoes." *Michigan Out-of-Doors* (December 1988): 64.

"For Those Who Gave the Family a Bad Name." *New York Times* (July 22, 1996).

Getchell, Dave. "Tubbs Snowshoes (Evaluation)." *Backpacker* (December 1991): 69.

Gonyea, Don, and Paul Eisenstein. "Making Tracks." *Michigan Business* (September 1988): 42.

Griffin, Steven A. "Snowshoe Clinic." *Midland (Michigan) Daily News* (February 12, 1997).

———. "Snowshoes: Time-Honored Winter Travel." *Michigan Living* (January 1983).

Hannon, Kerry. "Three Sizzling Ways to Hit the Slopes (Snowshoes, Snowboards, Hourglass Skis)." *U.S. News & World Report* (February 26, 1996): 76.

"Hot shoes for cold days." *Time* (January 7, 1991).

James, Sheryl. "Trade Snow Facts with Friends to Forget the White Outside." *Detroit Free Press* (January 10, 1997): 9a.

Jaques, Florence Page. *Snowshoe Country.* Illustrations by Francis Lee Jaques. Minneapolis: The University of Minnesota Press, 1944.

Kerasote, Ted. "Snow." *Sports Afield* (December 1992).

———. "Winter Moves: Skis or Snowshoes?" *Sports Afield* (February 1996): 26.

Kirk, Ruth. *Snow.* New York: William Morrow & Company, 1978.

Kreps, E. *Camp and Trail Methods: Interesting Information for All Lovers of Nature. What to Take and What to Do.* Columbus, OH: The A. R. Harding Publishing Co., 1910.

Lockhart, Gary. *The Weather Companion: An Album of Meteorological History, Science, Legend, and Folklore.* Wiley Science Editions. New York: John Wiley & Sons, 1988.

Lowie, Robert H. *Indians of the Plains.* 1954. Reprint. Lincoln, NE: University of Nebraska Press, Bison Books, 1982.

Mapes, Alan. "Snowshoes: Tools for Weathering the Winter." *Conservationist* (December 1994): 24.

McDowell, Edwin. "Women Abandon Nation's Ski Slopes." *New York Times* article, reprinted in *Detroit Free Press* (March 3, 1997).

McHugh, Tom. *The Time of the Buffalo.* 1972. Reprint. Lincoln, NE: University of Nebraska Press, Bison Books, 1979.

Nottingham, Suzanne. "Winter Terraining: Whether You're a Stroller or a Sprinter, Snowshoeing Is a Perfect Workout." *Skiing* (December 1995): 58.

O'Brien, Joan. "Superior: Pretty, Perilous; The Face of Danger." *Salt Lake Tribune* (January 26, 1997): J-1.

Opre, Tom. "Snowshoes Get You off the Beaten Path." *Detroit Free Press* (January 1, 1988).

Orr, R. B. "Snowshoes." *32nd Annual Archaeological Report*, Min. Ed., Toronto, Ontario, Canada (1920): 19–37.

Plueddeman, Charles, Michael Hodgson, F. H. Bernard, and Ted West. "Sporting Gear." *Outdoor Life* (January 1996): 67.

Redfeather. *Redfeather Revolutionizes Snowshoeing*. Backgrounder, 1997.

Silva. *Map and Compass Skills Guide*. Johnson Camping, 1992.

Ski Industries America. *Your Guide to Ski and Snowboard Apparel*. Brochure, 1997.

Ski Industries Association of America. *Lots of Ways to Enjoy Yourself on Snow*. News release, 1995.

———. *Ski, Sled, Skate or Shoe: Equipment Provides Lots of Snow Fun*. News release, 1996.

———. *Snowshoeing: The Trendiest Winter Activity*. News release, 1996.

———. *To Those Headed for the Slopes: Don't Leave Home Without. . . .* News release, 1996.

Smith, Edmund Ware. "How to Relax on Webbed Feet." *Ford Times* (January 1962): 25.

Smith, Richard P. *Animal Tracks and Signs of North America: Recognize & Interpret Wildlife Clues*. Harrisburg, PA: Stackpole Books, 1982.

Spilner, Maggie. "Snowshoes for Winter Wellness." *Prevention* (February 1995): 120.

Thomas, Paul. "Adventure Afoot." *Traverse, the Magazine* (January 1989).

Tubbs. "Snowshoeing: A 'Hot' Winter Sport on the Move." News release.

University of California. "Snowshoes: Walking through Winter." *Berkeley Wellness Letter* (January 1995): 6.

Wagner, Ronald L., and Bill Adler, Jr. *The Weather Sourcebook: Your One-Stop Resource for Everything You Need to Feed Your Weather Habit*. Old Saybrook, CT: The Globe Pequot Press, 1994.

Whitney, Stephen T. "Snowshoes for Every Need." *Vermont Life* (Winter 1967).

Williams, Jack. *The Weather Book: An Easy-to-Understand Guide to the USA's Weather*. New York: Random House, Vintage Books, 1992.

Zoellner, Tom. "Healthy and Grateful, Slide Survivor Realizes: 'It Wasn't My Time to Go.'" *Salt Lake Tribune* (January 27, 1997): D-1.

Index